DIVINE QUIETNESS

DIVINE QUIETNESS

FINDING MEANING WHEN HEAVEN IS SILENT

Emily Robison Adams

DESERET BOOK
SALT LAKE CITY

© 2023 Emily Robison Adams

All rights reserved. No part of this book may be reproduced in any form or by any means without permission in writing from the publisher, Deseret Book Company, at permissions@deseretbook.com. This work is not an official publication of The Church of Jesus Christ of Latter-day Saints. The views expressed herein are the responsibility of the author and do not necessarily represent the position of the Church or of Deseret Book Company.

DESERET BOOK is a registered trademark of Deseret Book Company.

Visit us at deseretbook.com

Library of Congress Cataloging-in-Publication Data
(CIP data on file)
ISBN 978-1-63993-122-4

Printed in the United States of America
PubLitho, Draper, UT

10 9 8 7 6 5 4 3 2 1

To those who walked with me

Contents

Quietness 1

Doubt 6

Rethinking 17

Quietness, Rethought 31

God's Will 45

Faith, Rethought 56

Spiritual Nourishment 64

The Body of Christ 81

Foundation 92

Acknowledgments 103

Notes 105

Works Cited 113

Quietness

I have asked God many direct questions in my life: Is the Church true? Is Joseph Smith a prophet? Do you love me? Is the Book of Mormon true? Should I marry Lucas? Should I have a child now? I've decided to attend law school; is that the direction I should go?

These are commonly asked questions, questions that inquire about the truthfulness of our spiritual life and the direction of our physical life. But I have not received an answer for most of these questions, at least an answer that fell into the category of what I believed was typical of revelation: a feeling in the heart, words in the mind, or phrases in scripture that jumped off the page.

Throughout my teenagerhood, twenties, and early thirties, I asked questions in a variety of ways. I would fast, attend the temple, wait on my knees until kneeling got uncomfortable, get out my journal and prepare to write, frame and reframe the questions hoping that a different way of asking would get an answer. Any answer. With one exception, the typical answers never came. After asking a question several ways, I would assume that divine silence meant assent or at least not disapproval. So I moved forward. I chose to believe in the Book of Mormon, in a loving God, and in a restored church. I married Lucas, had children, and went to law school.

Even still, my inability to receive answers to direct questions bothered me, even though I felt that I had an otherwise thriving spiritual life. I often felt the Spirit, I had flashes of inspiration when I was preparing a lesson or a talk, I had promptings to reach out to individuals, and I found delight in the scriptures. But when President Russell M. Nelson emphasized the necessity of receiving personal revelation,[1] I keenly perceived a gap in my ability to obtain that revelation. Receiving answers to direct questions seemed like a foundational piece of personal revelation, and I was terrible at it. I decided to figure out how I could get answers to direct questions.

I decided to pray for a revelation that would be easy for God to give: Is the Book of Mormon true? I had acted on Moroni's promise before—prayed about whether the book was true—but I had not received an answer. I had sat through many church meetings where members testified that they took Moroni's promise and prayed, and they felt that the Book of Mormon was true. I thought that trying to get a direct answer from God on the truthfulness of the Book of Mormon was a righteous desire and thus had a high likelihood of being answered.

To increase my chances of getting an answer, I read the entire Book of Mormon in about six weeks' time. And at the beginning of a new year, I knelt down and prayed. I asked God for a manifestation from the Holy Ghost that the Book of Mormon was true. I waited on my knees, hoping for some feeling, some warmth, some rumbling, some . . . something. Nothing came. After waiting, I decided that God needed me to ask more, so I kept asking.

I prayed for a few weeks with the same results. My prayers

became more earnest and tearful than they had ever been. I pleaded; I poured out; I did everything I thought I needed to do. But I did not feel anything. I heard nothing. I felt nothing. I sat in silence. The answer to my earnest prayers about the Book of Mormon was divine quietness. And in addition to the silence I felt on this question, my normal spiritual life also went quiet. The Spirit seemed to have disappeared. God felt gone.

For a time, I was in denial: maybe God wasn't really gone; perhaps I was still praying incorrectly, or maybe I didn't need an answer, or maybe God was too busy. At times I felt angry—angry at God for not answering, angry at myself for believing in such a God, and angry at the scriptures for teaching that God would answer. I did bargain some. I bought lots of books with the hope that if I hit the right book or figured out how to do the right thing, God would come back and I could feel the Spirit again. Coloring all of this was brain-pounding anxiety and a significant depression that creeped in a few months after the quietness started. After some therapy, I realized what I was feeling was grief. I felt that I had lost God.

It is embarrassing to admit that what triggered my faith struggle was God not answering my prayers about the truthfulness of the Book of Mormon in a way that I could recognize, which led to my spiritual life going dark. Prior to this quietness, I believed that if I had any spiritual gift, it was the gift of faith. I preached that faith was a choice. Even though there were times I had struggled with certain topics or policies or facets of history, I had chosen to keep the faith. But when I experienced divine quietness, my faith crumbled. That nonanswer seemed like a small thing in the context of an entire life of faith that, in my case, had been punctuated with sweet experiences with God. In my mind, faithful people didn't have their faith crumble over something so little. Nor did faithful people experience divine quietness, because that was reserved for those who committed some sin that chased away the Spirit or had lazy spiritual practices. I thought I was a faithful person, but here I was, stuck in a space of divine quietness triggered by a lack of an answer to a prayer. That was reality.

About one year after the quietness started, I slowly—almost imperceptibly—stopped fighting against it and started accepting it. Of course, I still felt anger and depression at times. I frequently wished that I could find the one right thing that would magically make everything work again. But I started playing with the idea that I was acceptable to God in my doubting, angry, bargaining, and depressed stages. Perhaps I could accept a God who occasionally did go quiet. Maybe I could learn something in this quietness that I could not have learned had God answered.

The divine quietness brought with it doubt. Although the doubt, for some time, was pointed at God, eventually it turned inward and exposed the assumptions I had made about God and my spiritual life. I realized I had internalized the assumption that God was, in many ways, formulaic—that if I did certain things, God would respond in certain ways. I learned the value of rethinking the assumptions I held that had invisibly animated my faith but could not withstand real-life experience. The collapse of those assumptions collapsed my faith. I slowly learned that the collapse was a gift. With those assumptions gone, I could explore the foundation for my faith in God. I could begin to get comfortable with uncertainty and with a faith based on love and the goodness of God, detached from my expectations of how God should show up in my life.

I started reading widely. I connected with a small group of

friends who had felt similar quietness, although the triggers for their quietness were different than mine. As I began to open up to my family, my mother suggested that I write down my experience. I thought that was a good idea—once I had figured out everything and knew the answers. But the answers did not come easily, if at all. A few months later, I started writing, hoping that the wrestle inherent in the writing process would bring clarity. Perhaps I could find healing in this experience if I did the work of putting it on paper.

This book, then, is simply a compilation of what I am learning. I hope that it is helpful for those who find themselves in similar circumstances. What I have needed to do has been different than what my friends—who were experiencing similar doubt and quietness—needed to do. Each of us walked our own path, but we could lean on and learn from each other. This is a book about my experience; it is unique to me. Please take what is helpful and leave the rest.

Doubt

When I first felt divine quietness, I was surprised but tried to shoulder that surprise with faith. As the quietness continued, I started to doubt. My doubts pricked at the nature of God and my relationship to God. My doubts were painful. Even more painful were reminders to not doubt, that faith could not exist with doubt, and that doubt was the product of some sin or ineffectiveness on my part. It was challenging to deal with the doubts when I felt that I should not be having doubts at all.

In fact, I remember talking with some friends about doubts. With one friend, we wondered if we would be worthy of temple recommends because we were in a doubting space: could we say that we had faith in God if we doubted that God was loving and even interested in us? With another friend, we discussed whether the feelings we were having were more question-like or doubt-like, and with some disappointment we realized they were more like doubts. Against the backdrop of directions to not doubt, we wondered what we should do with our doubts. Dismissing them did not solve our problems and labeling them as bad—because they were doubts and not questions—left us feeling ashamed and unworthy. We were unable to grapple with our doubts because we were burdened with the idea that doubts are antithetical to faith.

My concerns about doubt stemmed from the many scriptural directives to not doubt: "Doubt not, but be believing" (Mormon 9:27); "Look unto me in every thought; doubt not, fear not" (Doctrine and Covenants 6:36); "Have faith, and doubt not" (Matthew 21:21).[1]

But among these directives to not doubt is a beautiful story about Jesus coming to us *even if* we doubt.

After Jesus had the miraculous experience of being transfigured on top of a mountain, he left the mountain and reentered the messiness of life, first encountering the scribes questioning his disciples, surrounded by a group of people (see Mark 9:14–16). Jesus learned that a father had asked the disciples to heal his sick son, but the disciples could not do the healing (see Mark 9:17–18). Jesus responded—although it is not clear to whom he is speaking—"O faithless generation, how long will I be with you? How long will I endure you? Bring him to me" (Wayment, Mark 9:19).

The father brought his son to Jesus and said, "But if you are able, help us and have compassion on us" (Wayment, Mark 9:22). Jesus responded, "If you are able? All things are possible for the one who believes" (Wayment, Mark 9:23). The father answered, "I believe. Help my unbelief" (Wayment, Mark 9:24). After Jesus heard this, he healed the son (see Mark 9:25–28).

What is interesting about Jesus's response to the father's request— "If you are able? All things are possible for the one who believes"—is that it seems calculated to draw out of the father the true state of his belief. Jesus did not heal the son until *after* the father had recognized his doubts.

Oftentimes the first step to wrestling with doubt is acknowledging our unbelief, even if it is painful. When we have doubts that trouble us, rather than shoving them into a box and pretending they do not exist, it is healthier to acknowledge them. Doubts that simmer under the surface, suppressed and ignored, all the while slowly percolating into how we think and feel, seem to be more harmful than doubts that are brought to God and given the benefit of some sunshine and careful thought. We cannot honestly engage with our doubts until we acknowledge their existence without shame. Along these lines, Elder Jeffrey R. Holland has counseled to "be as candid about your questions as you need to be" while at the same time being "true to the faith you *do* have."[2]

Importantly, Jesus did not shame this father when he asked for help with his unbelief. Jesus did not quiz the father or suggest that what little belief the father had was insufficient. Instead, Jesus simply healed the son. Once the father could acknowledge his unbelief and his desire to believe, Jesus got to work. The father's vocal recognition of his conflicting feelings gave space for Jesus to engage in his healing work.

Although unbelief was not a barrier to Jesus helping the father, unbelief was a barrier in other parts of Jesus's ministry. For example, when Jesus visited his hometown, those who knew him were astonished at his wisdom and said, "Is not this the son of the carpenter? Is not his mother named Mary, and are his brothers Jacob, Joseph, Simon, and Judas? And his sisters, are they not all with us? From where does he know all these things?" (Wayment, Matthew 13:55–56). Those people were "offended" at Jesus (see Wayment, Matthew 13:57). Jesus "did not do many miracles in that place because of their unbelief" (Wayment, Matthew 13:58).

Both the father and the people in Jesus's hometown struggled with unbelief. But the difference between the two—and perhaps one reason why Jesus could do miracles for one and not the other—was that the father asked Jesus for help with his unbelief, whereas the people in his hometown merely expressed incredulity. The father wanted to believe and brought his doubts to God; the people in Jesus's hometown were unwilling to believe and held their doubts tightly.

I wanted to be like the father. I wanted to believe. I wondered if I could, like the father, connect with Jesus even in my doubt.

The question, then, was what to do with my doubt. Elder Dale G. Renlund has said, "Doubt is not wrong unless it becomes an end in and of itself."[3] This type of doubt is "stagnant doubt." When in stagnant doubt, a person is "content with himself, unwilling to make the appropriate effort, to pay the price of divine discovery, [and] inevitably reaches unbelief and darkness. His doubts grow like poisonous mushrooms in the dim shadows of his mental and spiritual chambers."[4]

The question for me was how to approach my doubt in a way so that it would not stagnate.

I found guidance in the writing of Brian McLaren. During his twenty-four years as a pastor, he experienced an "intense period of faith deconstruction."[5] Not only did he wrestle with his own doubts, he helped members of his congregation work through their doubts, and he now works with pastors, priests, and other religious leaders who struggle with their faith.

He proposed that a life of faith can cycle through four stages. Not all individuals go through all four stages; in fact, many stay in the first two stages their entire lives and have fulfilling spiritual experiences. However, for those of us who do travel through all four stages, having a framework to think about faith and doubt can make the journey more bearable.

The first stage is called Simplicity "because it revolves around a simple mental function of sorting nearly everything into one of two categories."[6] We learn early "to put everything into two simple bins: good/bad, like/dislike, familiar/unfamiliar, us/them, male/female, in/out."[7] This is also the stage where we trust, depend on, and obey authority figures.[8] In Simplicity, we are highly committed to our faith, are focused on being in the right group and doing the right things, are certain about God, and believe in absolute rights and wrongs.

When we begin to itch at some of the rigidness in Simplicity, we move to Stage Two: Complexity. Complexity "is about pragmatism and independence."[9] In Complexity, we see authority figures more as coaches or mentors, and we see life as a complex game where we need to master skills and competencies.[10] In our faith, we value succeeding and being effective; we believe we can figure anything out if we approach things in the right way, using specific steps; we are enthusiastic and idealistic about learning.

However, when we do not see the results we were promised even though we followed all the rules, our "confidence cracks like a breached hull, [and] the doubts pour in."[11] We move to Stage Three: Perplexity. In Perplexity, we discover that some things about our faith are "messy, and far less confidence-inspiring than [we had] always been taught."[12] We work in a realm of doubt, deconstruction, and suspicion.[13] We value authenticity, honesty, reality, and critical thinking. Although we can cultivate the gifts of "humility, openness, curiosity, scholarship, and a commitment to understanding the truth, no matter the cost,"[14] we can also feel rudderless, disillusioned, cynical, nihilistic, and relativistic.[15]

But if we can turn the skepticism of Perplexity away from God and toward our understanding of God, we can reach Stage Four: Harmony. In Harmony, "we learn to hold binaries in larger unities, to gather paradox and tension in a larger embrace, to welcome diversity without division, to hear difference without dissonance."[16] Interestingly enough, this is not a stage where we find all the answers to our questions. Rather, we learn to hold "knowing and unknowing" together as "complements" rather than "opposites."[17] We learn to live in uncertainty and paradox, and it points us towards universal love.[18]

When I read McLaren's book, I was in the depths of Perplexity, and cynicism was setting in. McLaren's four stages gave me some much-needed hope, because they recast doubt as a natural part of a life of faith.

I looked back at my life and saw how my thinking patterns and beliefs fell into Simplicity and then evolved into Complexity in my teenagerhood and early twenties. In Complexity, I learned as much as I could. I believed that if I followed certain steps, then I could achieve certain results. But when those steps did not work for me multiple times when I asked God direct questions—and when they catastrophically failed (in my mind) when I asked for a witness of the truthfulness of the Book of Mormon—I plunged headlong into Perplexity.

In Perplexity, I doubted everything. I wondered if God was loving or terrible. I read the scriptures and saw a wrathful God meting out punishments. Church constantly reminded me of my faith deficit. I felt worthless. And I wondered if my spiritual life up to that point had been more imagined than real.

I stewed in Perplexity for months and months. But with the newfound realization that Perplexity was a normal and natural part of a life of faith, the balance of my doubts began to shift. I cannot explain why or how or exactly when it happened. My doubts had leaned heavily on the side of disbelieving in a loving God and wondering if God was just some arbitrary and wrathful ruler of the universe. But at some point, my doubts began to tip away from doubting God towards doubting *my understanding* of God. I began to think about how I thought about God.

"There's a difference between doubting God and doubting my understanding of God," wrote McLaren, "just as there's a difference between trusting God and trusting my understanding of God."[19] I began to realize that God exists outside of the stories I tell about God. God exists outside of my thoughts or understanding about God. God is God, and my thoughts about God are my thoughts about God. But it is easy to confuse the two.

Imagine God standing on a hill, beckoning me to come. Sometimes I approach God and actually touch God; I can connect with the real, actual God. But often, I approach God and instead of touching God, I erect a board next to him—an idea of what God is—and I touch that instead. I build on that board, adding a frame, a roof, walls, and stairs, and before I know it, when I approach God, I see a gazebo of ideas that I have built about God. I can still see God through the cracks, but God is covered by the way I have framed my beliefs and assumptions about God.

At first, that gazebo is a beautiful, strong structure, one that I am proud of. It sparkles in the sun. I can show it off to my neighbors. But then I notice that the roof is beginning to sag and the walls cannot hold the weight of the weather. Perhaps the gazebo is not as strong as I thought. More importantly, it is blocking me from interacting with the Being inside of it. Once I see the gazebo as an impediment, my job is to take it down, board by board, so that I can eventually touch the God who stands inside.

By separating my thoughts about God from God, the scriptures on not doubting can be read a little differently. For example, Thomas Wirthlin McConkie analyzed the scripture: "Look unto me in every thought; doubt not, fear not" (Doctrine and Covenants 6:36). He noted that in this scripture, we can distinguish between small-f *faith* and big-F *Faith*. Small-f *faith* is the way we frame our ideas about God. But big-F *Faith* is what he calls transcendent Faith, or Faith in Divinity.[20] Sometimes we confuse our small-f *faith* with big-F *Faith*: "The story we tell about experience comes to replace the actual experience."[21] What I think about God becomes God; the gazebo becomes God. When that happens, McConkie encourages us to doubt our small-f *faith*—our own understanding of God and the way we have framed our beliefs—without "doubt[ing] the reality of the Divine."[22] We should recognize that our experiences with "Faith (direct communion with the Absolute) [should] evolve our faith (our beliefs and thoughts) continually in response."[23]

Along these lines, President Dieter F. Uchtdorf pleaded, "Please, first doubt your doubts before you doubt your faith."[24] Allow God to be loving and worthy of worship. But take the 10,000-foot view on your doubts: examine them, consider the assumptions underlying them, think about the information you are missing, recognize your biases, and acknowledge your frame of mind.

Admittedly, my doubt went beyond doubting my understanding of God and went straight to doubting God. I had thoroughly confused my ideas about God with the actual God. I had hidden God inside a gazebo of my ideas, and I could no longer see him. After I realized that, I slowly moved to a space where I could examine my ideas and was willing to let them go.

Rather than my doubts being a death knell to my faith (which they certainly felt like for several months), my doubts became the lens through which I could see the assumptions, ideas, and philosophies that had animated my faith but simultaneously crowded out God. This kind of doubt, Adam Miller wrote, "is a strong solvent that can burn holes in your stories and lead you back to the work of being faithful to life and, thus, to God."[25] This type of doubt "dislocates us from our comfortable places,"[26] writes Patrick Mason, and can spark "deeper spiritual yearnings and more mature reflection on the complexities of mortality."[27]

I am learning that I can view my doubts through the lens of a God who can "make 'all things'—including my doubts—'work together for good,'" as Mason writes.[28] And I am learning that, as Thomas McConkie wrote, "it is not by banishing doubt that we ultimately resolve the tension with faith, but by bringing the two into a deeper synthesis. . . . If properly supported, this doubt will open us to new revelation by clearing out old cherished beliefs to make room for more profound truths."[29]

I now view doubt like the eye. The eye sees clear images when light enters the eyeball and focuses directly onto the retina. Most of us are born with eyeballs that refract light directly onto the retina, so we can see crisp images. Over time, some eyeballs change shape, or the curve on the front of the eyeball—the cornea—changes. That change comes at different times of life, and it generally is a result of natural causes: genetics. When that happens, light does not focus directly on the retina; rather, the light focuses on a different part of the eye, causing images to appear blurry.

Once the shape or curve of an eyeball has changed, no amount of ignoring or willpower will get the eye to permanently refract the light properly. As a person who reluctantly got glasses in fourth grade, I can say that no amount of squinting solves the problem. Instead, squinting is exhausting. The eyes get tired. The brain gets tired. The old ways of seeing do not work. The only way to see a clear image again is to wear corrective lenses so that the light is refracted differently into the eye. And the strength and prescription for those lenses is unique to the shape and curvature of each eye.

So, too, with doubt. Once doubt changed the shape of my faith, I saw things differently than I did before. Ignoring the doubt strained my faith, because I was trying to force my faith to look like it did before. But that earlier stage of faith was gone. Wallowing in doubt also was unhelpful; not seeing clearly (or thinking clearly) is frustrating and, quite frankly, reduces our quality of life. What I am learning to do is accept that I have doubts and embark on the journey of finding the lenses that help me see clearly again. Those lenses often involve grace, different ways of thinking, or a broader understanding of a complex issue. I may have to try a variety of lenses before I find one that works. Those lenses may only work for a short period of time before I have to replace them. But when I find the lenses that work for me at that moment, I see things that I have not seen clearly in a long time—or perhaps ever.

Doubt, then, does not have to be destructive to faith. Rather, it can prompt us to ask questions and consider viewpoints that were never on our radar. It can encourage us to reexamine our assumptions about ourselves, about church, and about God. And hopefully, in that process, we can see differently—perhaps more clearly—than we did before.

Rethinking

President Russell M. Nelson declared that the Lord is "inviting us to change our mind, our knowledge, our spirit—even the way we breathe. He is asking us to change the way we love, think, serve, spend our time, treat our [spouses], teach our children, and even care for our bodies."[1] Our God is one who repeatedly asks us to assess where we are and move closer to him. This is a God who invites thinking and rethinking.

But rethinking is not easy, especially when the rethinking involves faith and doubt. In my case, turning my doubts *away from* God and *toward my understanding* of God was disconcerting. We often change our possessions and our wardrobes, psychologist Adam Grant wrote, but "when it comes to our knowledge and opinions, though, we tend to stick to our guns. . . . We favor the comfort of conviction over the discomfort of doubt, and we let our beliefs get brittle long before our bones."[2] That is because "reconsidering something we believe deeply can threaten our identities, making it feel as if we're losing a part of ourselves."[3]

This was especially true of my ideas about God. I preferred sticking to the ideas of God I had learned decades earlier. Those ideas were familiar. And they were comfortable because they made God predictable and controllable.

Reconsidering those ideas brought discomfort. I felt unsure and anchorless. Who was I if my idea of God was wrong? What did my life look like? Was there any meaning in any of it? This questioning came with a sense of loss. Over time, I had to learn to be willing to let go, to grieve what I lost, and to open my mind to other ideas that contained more truth than the ones I had been grasping previously.

In this process, I found myself—for a lack of better descriptors—having periods of hardening and softening.

In the hardening periods, I was unwilling to listen to new information, and I threw out anything that was in tension with what I currently thought. I felt hardening at the beginning of the quietness, because I refused to think that God would go quiet. And when I had to admit that God had gone quiet, I hardened again, refusing to believe that God answered prayers and was loving.

In those hardened periods, I could not wrestle with these thoughts, because I was not willing to entertain the idea that I had been (or currently was) wrong. This, I learned, is a very natural response to information that challenges core beliefs. As Grant notes, "When our core beliefs are challenged, it can trigger the amygdala, the primitive 'lizard brain' that breezes right past cool rationality and activates a hot fight-or-flight response. The anger and fear are visceral: it feels as if we've been punched in the mind. The totalitarian ego comes to the rescue with mental armor."[4] The job of the totalitarian ego is "to keep out threatening information."[5] If my totalitarian ego was in control, no wonder I was unable to wrestle with my doubts and question my ideas.

Much of this hardness—this inability to accept new information and engage with my ideas and doubts—stemmed from a significant depression and anxiety that started a few weeks after the quietness started. When God went quiet, I felt I had lost God. I also thought that God's quietness meant that I was worthless or, at the very least, unworthy or clueless about how to communicate with God. All of these feelings led to a profound sadness, deeper than I had ever experienced. That was depression. The anxiety came later, when I began to believe that God would only come back if I did something that required extreme personal sacrifice. I walked around feeling deeply afraid of what God would require of me. It took me months to realize I was feeling depression and anxiety, months to realize that I could not deal with them on my own, and months more to get an appointment with medical providers.

I felt ridiculous admitting to my providers that I was seeing them because I was experiencing an existential crisis. I was confused and felt abandoned by God, and those feelings did not stem from personal trauma, such as struggles with my spouse, parents, children, work, or health (in my mind, those were "real issues" that should land you in therapy). Since this struggle was just spiritual, shouldn't I handle it on my own? The answer for me was no; I needed help. Thankfully, my providers treated me with kindness. They did not discount my spiritual crisis as trivial.

Quite possibly the most powerful thing my providers did for me was validate my feelings. In my first session, my therapist told me that feeling like I had lost God *was* hard, especially since God had been a significant piece of my life. She said we would work through the grief together. She helped me pinpoint the thoughts that were triggering my anxiety, and together we discussed why those thoughts could be inaccurate. She gave me tools to challenge those thoughts. My medical provider approached the situation similarly: she validated how I felt and emphasized to me that my struggles were no more or less important than another person's. We talked about brain chemistry and medication and lifestyle changes. I started exercising more regularly, because that helped me feel less anxious and depressed. I began to understand the benefits of self-care and took it more seriously. And I started on medication, which enabled me to actually implement the things I was learning.

About one year after the quietness started—after I had done some therapy and started on medication—I began to recover. I learned that recovering from depression and anxiety does not necessarily mean feeling happy and calm (and totally spiritual) all the time; rather, the goal is to learn to think more accurately. As my brain moved out of a stage of being in constant panic and deep sadness, I felt that I could face my doubts, hear things that were hard, and wrestle with it all. Rather than avoiding, diving under the covers when things were hard (or feeling apathetic), I was willing to engage.

Being willing to engage with my doubts—and information that challenged my doubts—was the first step to softness and openness. I began to learn to respond to my spiritual confusion with curiosity rather than despair.

In the process of figuring out how to be open, I heard a speech by astrophysicist Neil deGrasse Tyson on the scientific method. Although I am not suggesting that the scientific method is the way to find spiritual truth, I found some of the scientific processes helpful in my spiritual rethinking.

In his speech, Tyson described the scientific method as doing "whatever it takes to not fool yourself into thinking something is true that is not or to thinking that something is not true that is."[6] To him, the scientific method is not linear and direct; rather, it is messy, sometimes circuitous, and filled with paths that dead-end. And because nature is the ultimate judge of whether an experiment will work or not, a scientist should use "methods and tools that allow nature to manifest in whatever way it can to give you the guidance to wherever the truth lies."[7]

To illustrate this point, Tyson pointed to the orbits of Uranus, Mercury, and Neptune.

The laws of planetary motion and gravity were developed by Isaac Newton in the 1600s. In the late 1700s, an astronomer discovered Uranus, but its orbit was not obeying Newton's laws. Faced with Uranus's noncompliant orbit, the scientific community had either found the limits of Newton's laws—or had not yet discovered another object in space that was pulling on Uranus's orbit and that pulling could be explained by Newton's laws. Astronomers did the calculations under Newton's laws as if another object existed beyond Uranus, and they found one: Neptune. In this case, Newton's laws were correct once the astronomers saw the entire picture. By seeing Uranus without Neptune, Uranus's orbit defied Newton's laws; by seeing Uranus with Neptune, Uranus's orbit followed Newton's laws. Sometimes, the scientific laws are correct; we just don't have a complete picture.

But other times, the scientific laws have limits, as was the case with Mercury. Like Uranus, Mercury's orbit was not following Newton's laws. Based on their experience with Uranus, astronomers believed that another planet closer to the sun was pulling on Mercury. So astronomers started looking for that planet but could not find it. Eventually, Albert Einstein developed his general theory of relativity that changed our understanding of gravity. Although Newton's laws still worked, they worked—according to the theory of relativity—with moons and planets, but those laws broke down when it came to the sun. When Einstein's theory of relativity was applied to Mercury, Mercury did exactly what the theory of relativity said it was supposed to do. Sometimes the laws that have withstood scrutiny for hundreds of years hit something the laws cannot explain, and the laws need to be reexamined.

But sometimes we have the law right, and we just have bad data. Such was the case with Neptune.

After its discovery, astronomers discovered that Neptune's orbit was not obeying Newton's laws, and it was too far away from the sun for Einstein's theory of relativity to apply. So astronomers started looking for another planet that could be pulling on Neptune's orbit, just as Neptune had pulled on Uranus's orbit. Eventually, astronomers found Pluto. But their calculations did not make sense: Pluto wasn't in the right place and wasn't large enough to be affecting Neptune's orbit. A scientist then pulled the data from the relevant observatories and found that one observatory's data didn't seem correct, as if an instrument hadn't been calibrated correctly. The scientist removed that observatory's data and recalculated, and found that Neptune's orbit was doing exactly what Newton's laws said it was supposed to do. Sometimes bad data mucks everything up.

Figuring out why each of these orbits looked a certain way required different types of rethinking for each planet. Astronomers would never have discovered Neptune if they had ignored the idiosyncrasies in Uranus's orbit. They would never have thrown out bad data from Neptune unless they had looked at the data more carefully. And they would still be looking for that mysterious planet that was pulling on Mercury (according to Newton's laws) had they not rethought the limits of Newton's laws. With curiosity and a willingness to rethink, astronomers and scientists discovered new planets and articulated laws about gravity that more closely resembled how gravity actually works.

Notably, these thinkers did not confuse Newton's laws and Einstein's theory of relativity with actual gravity. Gravity exists in nature; gravity does not change because humans come up with laws or theories to describe it. Rather, those laws and theories are merely a way of describing the current human understanding of gravity. Those descriptions and understandings change over time, hopefully coming closer to a more complete and accurate description of gravity. And these laws and theories are up for rethinking when something in nature does not comport with our current understanding.

Of course, I don't think that I can scientific-method God to figure out who God is. But I love the curiosity, humility, and mental flexibility inherent in the method. What if I could look at my ideas of God as simply constructs that I had formed to describe God the best I could under my current understanding? Sometimes those constructs work well. When I hit something that doesn't make sense within that construct, if I am patient, I may discover something beyond my view that, if considered, works within the construct. On the other hand, sometimes those constructs completely break down—they work in one scenario but not another. So I have to rethink what my construct is and what its boundaries are. I have to reshape it. Sometimes the construct works well, but if I fill it full of inaccuracies, I end up with a distorted view of reality.

What if, when I see something that doesn't comport with my construct, I choose to be curious rather than completely collapsing and throwing out the constructs altogether? What if I could doubt my constructs and be willing to revise them, while at the same time holding fast to the hope that God does exist, and it was a worthwhile lifetime endeavor to get close to God? What if the goal is to not have the construct become God—I do not want to worship products of my own mind—but to revise and wrestle with my constructs in a way that brings me closer to God?

"It takes great humility," Thomas McConkie writes, "to continually reexamine our stories and challenge our own framing of things to see if we might arrive at something even more true."[8] In fact, C. S. Lewis acknowledged that God shatters our ideas of God, and that "shattering is one of the marks of His presence."[9] As two Christian thinkers have written, our "*ideas* of God are always at risk of being rendered obsolete by God's actual presence and activity in our lives."[10]

Being willing to rethink—being a little softer, more curious, more humble, and more flexible—allowed me to reexamine my beliefs and doubts. I had a core belief that God would respond in a certain way if I followed particular steps; when I felt hardened, I wanted to hold onto that belief with a tight fist, ignoring the experience I was having (God seemed to be quiet although I followed all the steps). Trying to suffocate my experience actually amplified the quietness, and there was so much dissonance between what I believed and what I was experiencing that collapse was inevitable. When I was deep in doubt, I oscillated between thoughts that God did not love me; I was unlovable; God was arbitrary and not worth worshipping; and everything I had believed was a hoax. The hardness I experienced as I grasped at a transactional God translated into a similar hardness as I waded through a terrible God.

It took time, many conversations, therapy, and medication to get me to a point where I was willing to ease the hardness I was feeling and become softer. Seeing my ideas and doubts about God simply as *my thoughts*—not the actual God—started that softening. And that began the rethinking process. For me, that rethinking was necessary for my spiritual survival.

When I look at the scriptures through the lens of rethinking, I see a God who consistently challenges human ideas of who God is supposed to be. In other words, I see a God who invites us to rethink.

Take Enoch, for example. God showed Enoch a remarkable vision of "things which were not visible to the natural eye" (Moses 6:36). Because of God's call, Enoch traveled around the land and "spake forth the words of God," preaching the doctrines of the creation, the fall, the atonement, baptism, repentance, justification, sanctification, and the plan of salvation (see Moses 6:43–63). He taught for a long period of time, "and so great was the faith of Enoch that . . . he spake the word of the Lord, and the earth trembled, and the mountains fled, even according to his command; and the rivers of water were turned out of their course; and the roar of the lions was heard out of the wilderness; and all nations feared greatly, so powerful was the word of Enoch, and so great was the power of the language which God had given him" (Moses 7:13). Enoch seems about as close to God as any prophet ever was.

But even though Enoch was intimately connected with God,

Enoch had gaps in his understanding of God. After he had done all this preaching, earth trembling, and mountain moving, he had another vision where he saw "the God of heaven look[ing] upon the residue of the people, and he wept" (Moses 7:28). Enoch was confused and asked God, "How is it that thou canst weep, seeing thou art holy, and from all eternity to all eternity?" (Moses 7:29).

Enoch then asked God an extended question, laying out his current understanding of God: "And were it possible that man could number the particles of the earth, yea, millions of earths like this, it would not be a beginning to the number of thy creations; and thy curtains are stretched out still; and yet thou art there, and thy bosom is there; and also thou art just; thou art merciful and kind forever; and thou hast taken Zion to thine own bosom, from all thy creations, from all eternity to all eternity; and naught but peace, justice, and truth is the habitation of thy throne; and mercy shall go before thy face and have no end; *how is it thou canst weep?*" (Moses 7:30–31; emphasis added).

Despite his close connection with God, Enoch had never thought that God could weep for his people. God challenged those ideas by showing Enoch a vision of a weeping God. He informed Enoch that because of the wickedness of the people, "the whole heavens shall weep over them . . . ; wherefore should not the heavens weep, seeing these shall suffer?" (Moses 7:37). Enoch learned—after years and years of preaching about and interacting with God—that God was a Being who was vulnerable and emotionally affected by the actions of his people.

The same rethinking happened to the brother of Jared. The brother of Jared was a man who was "highly favored of the Lord" (Ether 1:34). He prayed for God to preserve the language of his family and friends, and the Lord granted that request (see Ether 1:34–37). He asked God if his people should travel to another land, and in response, God said he would give his people a new land "because this long time ye have cried unto me" (Ether 1:43). God spoke with the brother of Jared in a cloud and gave him directions about where to go (see Ether 2:4–5). And several years later, God appeared to the brother of Jared again in a cloud and chastised him because he "remembered not to call upon the name of the Lord" and then gave him detailed instructions on how to build a boat (Ether 2:14–17). God was responsive to the brother of Jared and intimately involved in the details of his people's travel.

However, when the brother of Jared approached God in the boat-building process and asked God to put light into stones, the brother of Jared saw God's finger and was shocked (see Ether 3:6). The brother of Jared "knew not that the Lord had flesh and blood" (Ether 3:8). Even though the brother of Jared had been praying to God for years and received detailed instructions from God, he had never considered that God had a body.

Jesus's life is another example: He presented himself in a way that requires constant rethinking. Given the prophecies about a great Messiah, many were expecting Jesus to come in the form of a powerful military and political leader who would free the Jews from the oppression of the Roman Empire. But Jesus was not born to power or wealth. He was born to a poor family and was a refugee in Egypt for years as a young child. When he did enter the years of his ministry, he taught freedom from spiritual oppression. He was not the great military or political leader that the people had hoped for.

During his ministry, he frequently revised long-held beliefs. In his Sermon on the Mount, Jesus listed a series of well-settled beliefs starting with the phrase: "Ye have heard that it was said by them of old time . . ." (cf. Matthew 5:21, 27, 33, 38, 43). He then followed the well-settled belief with a "but I say unto you," revising the old belief. For example, Jesus taught: "*Ye have heard that it hath been said*, Thou shalt love thy neighbour, and hate thine enemy. *But I say unto you*, Love your enemies, bless them that curse you, do good to them that hate you, and pray for them which despitefully use you, and persecute you" (Matthew 5:43–44; emphasis added). Jesus took the old dichotomy of love and hate and turned it on its head. Love was no longer reserved for just our friends—it was something that we needed to feel for all of humanity. Jesus took a long-held belief and rethought it.

Beyond his family circumstances and the Sermon on the Mount, Jesus showed up throughout his life in ways that challenged ideas about how God should act. When a woman was accused of being caught in adultery, he sidestepped the Mosaic law—which emphasized justice (stoning in this instance)—and invited those around him to examine their own hearts (see John 8:3–11). He spoke with the Samaritan woman at the well—something a Jewish man should not do—and in the book of John, she was the first person (not Jesus's disciples) to know of Jesus's Messianic calling (see John 4:1–26). When the woman with the issue of blood touched his clothes, he responded in kindness and told her that her faith had made her whole (see Matthew 9:20–22). If she had been bleeding while she touched him, she would have been ritually unclean and would have made Jesus ritually unclean, but Jesus did not shy away from her touch or chastise her for making him ritually unclean (see Leviticus 15:19).[11]

Through these actions, Jesus challenged ideas about how God

interacted with women (in contrast to the extant culture, he valued women rather than diminished them), with those who were not Jewish (Jesus welcomed all regardless of their pedigree), and with those who were ritually unclean (fear of ritual uncleanliness did not prevent him helping those in need). His actions pushed those around him to rethink how they treated people that were frequently categorized as not worthy of God's time or love.

One final example: during the Last Supper, Jesus started to wash his disciples' feet—a dirty job that was left for servants. When Jesus came to Peter, Peter refused Jesus's service (see John 13:8). Perhaps Peter was uncomfortable with the idea that God would do servant's work or touch the dirtiest part of Peter's body. Whatever Peter's reasoning, his ideas about God made no room for Jesus to wash his feet. But Jesus pushed back at Peter, reminding him, "If I wash thee not, thou hast no part with me" (John 13:8). Peter had to allow Jesus to serve him. Jesus willingly interacts with the dirtiest, hardest parts of our souls. This is not the picture of an aloof, sovereign-like God who does not want to get his hands messy. Rather, Jesus pushed Peter to rethink what Jesus's role was: Jesus came to help and to serve. Peter had to allow Jesus to do what Jesus was already willing and ready to do. Peter had to reform his image of godliness.

For me, God invites rethinking, not only rethinking about myself and my behavior, but rethinking of my ideas about God. As I see in the stories of Enoch and the brother of Jared, God invites rethinking at all stages of my life, regardless of how much I thought I knew and how connected I thought I was. Rethinking invites me to embrace the very likely reality that I cannot know all of God. Rethinking allows me to accept that *not knowing* does not mean that I give up. Rather, it encourages me to be open to different ways that God can show up in my life and guide me. Rethinking pushes me away from Pharisaic rigidity to more mental and spiritual flexibility. The ensuing curiosity and humility bring courage to wrestle with my doubts and with my faith. And hopefully, all of this allows me to let go of inaccurate ideas about God and grow closer to the actual God who reigns in the heavens.

Quietness, Rethought

My first step in the rethinking process was to reconsider the meaning of divine quietness.

Before the quietness started, I had heard several explanations for why someone didn't receive an answer to prayer or feel the Spirit. One was lack of personal worthiness. And although that may be true in some instances, I did not feel that I lacked personal worthiness when I first experienced divine quietness. For me, the Spirit went quiet in the middle of my earnest prayers about the Book of Mormon, when I was also striving to live my covenants and attend the temple frequently. I had also heard that depression can dampen the feeling of the Spirit, but I sank into depression after I felt my spiritual life go quiet. The quietness triggered the depression.

There were descriptions of tuning into the right frequency to hear the Spirit, but I had no idea how to do that since I thought I was already doing everything right. Then there were reminders that I wasn't trying hard enough, so if I read more or prayed more or fasted more, I could feel something again. I did spend some time trying to do more; I bought a lot of books, hoping that the next one would hold the answer. But nothing described how I was feeling—what seemed like an intentional divine quietness—and nothing made it better. If anything, this frenetic push to figure out what was wrong with me left me feeling more frustrated and disillusioned. The traditional explanations for divine quietness did not seem to describe what I was experiencing.

Because I had never thought that divine quietness could be a refining experience, I spent a lot of time either denying the quietness, trying to find a quick way to get God back, pondering my worthiness, or questioning the nature and existence of God. I struggled to find something that explained how I was feeling. Certainly I had language to explain losing the Spirit because of poor life choices or lazy spiritual practices. But I did not have the vocabulary to understand what I viewed as *intentional* divine quietness and withdrawal—nor did I have the skills to navigate it.

In the scriptures, intentional divine quietness appears at some of the most painful moments. Joseph Smith, sitting in Liberty Jail for months, wrote, "O God, where art thou? And where is the pavilion that covereth thy hiding place?" (Doctrine and Covenants 121:1). The Psalmist writes, "Lord, why castest thou off my soul? why hidest thou thy face from me?" (Psalm 88:14). And after hours of suffering in Gethsemane, at the hands of the Romans, in Jewish councils, and on the cross, Jesus cried, "My God, my God, why hast thou forsaken me?" (Matthew 27:46). Sometimes God seems to go quiet, even during times when we desperately need him.

Many have offered explanations for divine quietness.

One explanation was that quietness was a stimulant for growth. Elder Richard G. Scott wrote, "Often He withholds an answer, not for lack of concern, but because He loves us—perfectly. He wants us to apply truths He has given us. For us to grow, we need to trust our ability to make correct decisions."[1] Terryl and Fiona Givens similarly proposed that because God intends to "make us as independent in our sphere as He is in His," we may need to "learn to act on the basis of what drives us from within, rather than what acts upon us from without. It may be for this reason that the heavens close from time to time, to give us room for self-direction."[2] In other words, divine quietness can be God's way of stepping back and asking, "What will you do now?"[3]

Not only could quietness stimulate growth, it could also develop attributes—patience, compassion, and gratitude—that mature when times are difficult. Those attributes can widen your circle of influence. When a person's relationship with God has been rich and fulfilled, the absence of that relationship brings greater understanding for those who struggle to connect with or have faith in God from the very start. Quietness may create opportunities to influence people who would otherwise be turned off to those who truthfully proclaim that God has never gone quiet in their lives.

Others view quietness as a way for us to accept God's will. President Dallin H. Oaks noted that "the Lord will speak to us through the Spirit in His own time and in His own way."[4] Although many may "believe that when they are ready and when it suits their convenience, they can call upon the Lord and He will immediately respond, even in the precise way they have prescribed," God's "revelation does not come that way."[5] Rather, that revelation comes in God's time.

Some viewed quietness as a training ground for consistency and discipline in spiritual practices. Lauren Winner wrote, "One of God's gifts to some of us is just not to be immediate, so that we have to undergo the kind of discipline necessary to have what others seem to have effortlessly."[6]

Others recognize divine quietness as an invitation into a different relationship with God, one that acknowledges the other's presence without needing communication. Patrick Mason wrote, "The most meaningful response to divine silence is to recognize that perhaps God values *communion* with us as much as he does direct *communication*—that being *with* us does not always entail talking *to us*."[7] Communion with God—that intimate sharing of feelings with God—can be done in silence, Richard Rohr proposes, because "silence is the only language spacious enough to include everything and to keep us from slipping back into dualistic judgments and divisive words."[8] Thus, when God answers a prayer with silence, God "may be inviting you to share this silence with him," notes Adam Miller.[9]

In rethinking quietness, some have urged to not reduce God to words or feelings; in other words, God is not just active in our lives because of what he says, or because we can feel the presence of the Holy Ghost. Rather, God—as the creator of the universe—can be active in our lives in a variety of ways. He can inspire those around us to reach out. He can influence nature to soothe our souls or teach us. Along these lines, the Givenses urge being more "open to the myriad ways in which God enacts, rather than articulates, His response."[10]

I thought these perspectives were refreshingly hopeful and realistic. They introduced me to ways to view quietness, not as God's abandonment or anger, but rather as the hand of a loving God being involved in my life in a way that I could never have supposed. I could see quietness as a way to stimulate growth, confirm agency,

QUIETNESS, RETHOUGHT

reaffirm God's will, promote discipline, invite communion, and practice openness to God's hand in my life.

There were two points of view, however, that resonated with me most: the concept of a dark night of the soul and the concept of withdrawal as a normal part of human and divine relationships.

First to the dark night of the soul. When I first started reading about quietness, I picked up a book about Mother Teresa, who experienced a lengthy period of divine quietness. Mother Teresa spent her life serving the poorest of the poor in India and around the world. Although she began her service feeling close to God, she experienced decades feeling a quiet heaven and a divine separation. In describing how she felt, Mother Teresa wrote: "Where is my faith?—Even deep down, right in, there is nothing but emptiness & darkness. . . . When I try to raise my thoughts to Heaven—there is such convicting emptiness that those very thoughts return like sharp knives & hurt my very soul.—Love—the word—it brings nothing.—I am told God loves me—and yet the reality of darkness & coldness & emptiness is so great that nothing touches my soul."[11]

Although Mother Teresa sought assistance from her spiritual leaders, she never discovered how to break the silence and the emotional distress that came with it. Over time, she accepted the quietness: "The only response to this trial is the total surrender to God and the acceptance of the darkness in union with Jesus."[12]

Mother Teresa's experience is heartbreaking; here was a woman who spent her life in the service of the poor, whose desire was to serve God, and who yearned to feel the love of God, but those feelings were absent. I don't know why Mother Teresa's divine quietness was so severe, but her book was a gift to me. She confirmed that distance from God is painful. She continued her mission through her decades of quietness by courageously holding onto her earlier experiences with God where she felt divinely directed to serve the poor. And although the quietness was an intense source of pain, she worked towards accepting it and trying to turn to Jesus, even though she did not feel much in return.

I learned that in the Christian tradition, what Mother Teresa experienced is sometimes called the "dark night of the soul." Some have described that dark night as "extreme aridity" where "one feels rejected and abandoned by God."[13] The dark night is an agonizing and bewildering process "because one wants only God and loves Him greatly but is unable to recognize one's love for Him. The virtues of faith, hope, and charity are severely tried. Prayer is difficult, almost impossible; spiritual counsel practically of no avail."[14]

I did not experience all that Mother Teresa did, but in the divine quietness I experienced, I certainly felt abandoned and rejected by God. I felt completely alone. I felt nothing, and no amount of work on my part or well-meant counsel seemed to change that. Such an experience seemed contrary to what a loving God would do. Rather, it seemed like an experience handed out by a god who was not worth worshipping.

For several months, I struggled with what to do. I wondered if I should leave God altogether: if God was going to treat me this way, then there was no way I was going to stay. But for a reason I cannot explain, there seemed to be a golden thread that connected me to heaven; I felt tied, and I felt compelled to stay and keep trying. Something hinted that throwing away the God and church I grew up with was not a choice I should make at that moment. I decided to stay.

But, to be honest, the staying was not pretty. I took up the mantra that if I could just show up, that was enough. If I could get myself into the church building and into the chapel, that was enough. If I could get myself to sit down in front of general conference, that was enough. Even if I needed to leave for a moment because what was said was painful to hear, I still showed up. I realized that walking the halls for a moment during a church meeting because I felt I could not stay in the meeting was enough, because I was in the building. I could open up my scriptures and read a few verses, even if when I read them all I saw was a wrathful god. I could say a prayer at night, even if it was along the lines of: "I'm here. Are you?" Just showing up was one of the only things I felt that I could do to demonstrate to God that I was still interested and trying, even if—to others—my efforts seemed minimal.

But sitting in that empty space for months showed me parts of myself that I did not know existed. As the Trappist monk Thomas Merton observed: "It is in this darkness, when there is nothing left in us that can please or comfort our own minds, when we seem to be useless and worthy of all contempt, when we seem to have failed, when we seem to be destroyed and devoured, it is then that the deep and secret selfishness that is too close for us to identify is stripped away from our souls."[15] Somehow, that darkness purifies the soul. Perhaps when the Spirit came more easily, I could cover up spiritual and personal assumptions; I could justify behavior or attitudes because, at some point during the week, I could feel the Spirit. But when I could feel nothing, all justification was gone. I could see myself truly. I could see my pride more blatantly. My judgment of others and of myself became more obvious. And I could begin to see what I actually believed about God, because no longer was that belief covered in warm feelings. I no longer went to church, read my scriptures, or said my prayers with any sort of feeling of peace or comfort. My spiritual practice brought with it feelings of emptiness and nothingness. I had to wrestle with whether I did those practices just to obtain those feelings, or if there was a deeper, more beautiful piece of those practices that I had been missing.

I had always equated the presence of God (or the Spirit) with feeling *something*—whether that was love, peace, assurance, or any other similar uplifting emotion. It was challenging to think of the possibility that God could be equally present when I was feeling nothing. Merton has gone so far as to say that although a "sense of peace may be a sign that we are united to God, it is still only a sign—an accident. The substance of the union may be had without any such sense, and sometimes when we have no feeling of peace or of God's presence He is more truly present to us than He has ever been before."[16] He cautions that "if we attach too much importance to these accidentals we will run the risk of losing what is essential, which is the perfect acceptance of God's will, whatever our feelings may happen to be."[17] In other words, the all-consuming focus on what I was *feeling* crowded out the all-important lessons I could learn from God in a quiet space. Feeling something is a gift, but the absence of feeling is not necessarily a curse. Rather, it can be an invitation to relate to God in a different way.

Thus, the dark night of the soul can be liberating. As Barbara Brown Taylor contemplated, "It is about freeing you from your ideas about God, your fears about God, your attachment to all the benefits you have been promised for believing in God."[18] All of these things are "substitutes for God" and "get in God's way."[19]

The dark night, then, is a process of stripping away unnecessary baggage—whether that baggage comes from personal assumptions or trauma, cultural expectations, or tradition. As Peter Enns writes, "Our false god is being stripped away, and we are left empty—with none of the familiar ideas of God that we create to prop us up. The dark night takes away the background noise we have created in our lives in order to prepare us to hear God's voice later on—in God's time."[20] I am learning to view divine quietness as a refining experience, as a tool God uses to clear out notions that clutter and weaken faith through the painful process of riveting my attention on what I wanted most but could not find: God.

Second is the concept of withdrawal as a normal part of human and divine relationships. Wendy Ulrich, a psychologist who also sits on the Relief Society general advisory council, examined the invitations in the scriptures for Israel to be married to God and wondered if having a good relationship with God was based on some of the principles of having a good marriage.[21]

In thinking about building a relationship with God, she examined research on the stages of long-term, successful, committed marriage relationships. According to the research, long-term successful marriages generally move through four stages: Honeymoon (where the couple publicly commit to each other and are idealistic), Power Struggle (where spouses realize that they are fundamentally different from each other and realize that they will not solve a significant number of their problems), Withdrawal (where the spouses feel that they are so different from each other that they might not be able to make it work), and Acceptance and Renewal (where the spouses accept each other's differences and choose to love and trust each other).[22]

She noted that our relationship with God may follow the same four stages.

The Honeymoon stage with God involves doctrine resonating deeply, public declarations of our faith, and possibly having powerful spiritual experiences.[23] For me, this occurred in my younger and early teenage years. I was baptized at eight, felt the Spirit powerfully during my confirmation, went to church and my youth activities as a teenager, participated in testimony meetings, found that the scriptures resonated with me, and generally felt that God was a moving and active force in my life.

Then came the Power Struggle. The Power Struggle stage with God can be triggered by conflict with a leader, issues with a calling, trouble with our families, discomfort over history or doctrine or policies, or many other things.[24] Because we begin to realize that many problems or questions are not fully resolvable on earth, we may think that we have chosen the wrong God or the wrong church. We think that the right God and the right church would not have these problems—or at least the problems would be resolvable.[25] In analogizing the Power Struggle stage with God to a similar stage in marriages, Ulrich wrote that in successful, long-term marriages, only about 31 percent of problems get fully resolved over the course of the marriage; "that means about 69 percent of marital problems [are] never fully resolved," and the spouses "simply learn to cope with them as best we can, or work around them, or lessen their intensity, or ignore them."[26]

In my case, my Power Struggle stage with God started in my late teens and early twenties, and it began with feeling confused and discontent about some of the ways gender is handled in the Church. Unlike the world that my mother and grandmothers grew up in, gender did not prevent me from attending schools or holding jobs or doing some recreational activities. However, in the church that I loved that was headed by the God that I loved, there were things that I could not do because I was a woman. I wrestled with that for years. My power struggles with God intensified when I kept trying to get direct answers from God on questions I found important and necessary for my personal and spiritual growth, and although I followed the steps I was taught, those answers did not come in a way I could recognize. God seemed to be different than the list-based, communicative, active God I thought he was. Or perhaps I was just inept at communicating with God.

Then came the Withdrawal stage. According to Ulrich, in the Withdrawal stage with God, "we feel like turning away from God" because we cannot "understand Him."[27] Ulrich analogized the Withdrawal stage to a long, boring part of a road trip, through a place that is not "even worth being awake for."[28] During that long, boring part, "distracting ourselves, playing games in our heads, taking breaks, and steady persistence all had their place."[29] In the end, we get through that part of the road trip by simply driving. But that long, boring part can also become a place of great pain and extremity. "In the throes of such extremities, it can be immensely challenging to just keep driving, or walking, with no assurance that we're even on the right road. When the journey hurts this much, it is understandable that we might start looking for exits to anyplace but here."[30]

When I read about the Withdrawal stage, I didn't want to admit that perhaps I had contributed to my distance from God. Was it possible that I had turned away from God because I felt that understanding and growing close to God was not something I could do? I began to see how, after the quietness started, I withdrew from God. I read my scriptures less and with less zeal and enthusiasm.

My prayers became empty. Although there were times when I did everything I could to frenetically connect with God, the purpose of those actions was to make myself feel better. Although it was painful to admit, I may have withdrawn from God because I felt that he had withdrawn from me.

I found hope, though, in Ulrich's acknowledgment that the Withdrawal stage can be long and painful, and sometimes all we can do is just drive through it—just like we would drive through a boring part of a road trip. We can't skip those boring parts; we have to go through them. And so much of the Withdrawal stage is just keeping the car on the road and moving. We don't need a fancier car or better gas or different traveling companions—we just need to keep driving in whatever car we have with our tires on the road.

The Withdrawal stage can be followed by the Acceptance stage. In the marriage context, that stage means that we accept our spouse for who he or she really is, even though our spouse is different than we originally thought, and choose to trust and move forward with our spouse.[31] According to Ulrich, the Acceptance stage with God follows these same lines. It may begin with "underwhelming declarations of faith or conviction, or only tentative reinvestment in living the gospel."[32] But this time, "we are more willing to live with the answers we do get and the inspiration that does come, even when they don't come on our timetable, in accordance with our opinions, or with the absolute certainty we thought we were entitled to."[33] This stage can bring deeper humility, more patience, and more trust in God.

For me, the Acceptance stage brought hope—there was a stage after Withdrawal where I could still be with God! But it was a stage I could reach only after I let go of my preconceived notions of who

God was and what he should do. I had to allow God to be God, even if I did not fully understand him. And I had to trust that God was worthy of trusting, even if he did not show up in the way that I wanted.

Taken together, the dark night of the soul and the stage-of-relationship framework helped me see divine quietness differently. With the concept of the dark night of the soul, I learned that God can intentionally (and lovingly) go quiet. The purpose of that quietness is to help us realize and then release our small ideas about God. It can also help us approach our spiritual life differently: instead of obeying the commandments or engaging in spiritual practices because we expect something from them, we obey and engage simply because we love God. And with the stage-of-relationship framework, I learned that periods of quietness can also be prolonged by me.

Frankly, I preferred the dark night of the soul concept for quite some time, because I wanted all the responsibility for the divine quietness to land solely on God's shoulders, not mine. I wanted to see myself as the star student who got put into a difficult, upper-level class without her knowing it. I liked viewing myself as a victim in some cosmic scheme that I had no control over. I did not want to admit that I played any role in my spiritual life going quiet. But when I read about the stage-of-relationship framework, I could see the Withdrawal stage as one that perhaps was prolonged by my disengagement with God—a disengagement that occurred because what I was experiencing did not fit into my ideas of how God should act.

These two frameworks helped me to see quietness as a normal part of a relationship with God, just like I could begin to see doubt as a normal part of a life of faith. Normalizing quietness (and doubt) helped me feel that I was no longer completely defective. And because quietness could be part of a normal relationship with God, I didn't need to obsessively worry when I hit that quietness. I could learn to just drive through it, even though the drive might be awful, and even though there were no clear answers about how the drive would end up.

I am grateful for those who have wrestled with quietness and articulated their thoughts on why quietness happens, and what it has meant to them. Because of these writers, I am learning to see quietness differently than I did before. I can see the possibility that God can go quiet. But a quiet God is not an angry God or a careless God or an arbitrary God. I can see that quietness can be an invitation to a deeper look at myself and at my relationship with God. I can see the possibility that my actions play a role in quietness without beating myself up.

When I began to see God in the quietness, I stopped resisting it and instead leaned into it. I saw the quietness creating more compassion, exposing the weaknesses of my faith, and calling me to deeper humility. It beckoned me to wrestle with questions and doubts that had settled under the surface of my faith that I had never addressed. And it challenged me to see God working in my life, although I could not feel it.

In my quietness, I could choose to see God as absent, silent, and aloof. Or I could choose to see quietness as a different way that God could relate to me. The latter choice brought more hope and meaning. Instead of talking about God "going silent," I chose to speak of God as "going quiet." And perhaps, if I did not resist the quietness, I could find God in that quiet space.

God's Will

As I began to see divine quietness as a way to expose my problematic ideas about God, one of the first ideas that came to the fore was that, deep down, I believed that if I did certain things, then God was obligated to respond to me in a certain way. Of course, I'd been taught that God worked within his own timetable and in his own way. But I also heard a lot of emphasis about God's promises if I did certain things and processes I could follow to repent or receive personal revelation or pray (or any other gospel principle). In many ways, these formulas were good: they reduced amorphous gospel principles down to concrete steps. And those formulas conveyed that God was not arbitrary, was responsive to my behavior, and was a keeper of promises.

Those formulas became problematic when I slowly turned God into a formulaic God—if I do *a*, then God will do *b*. In other words, I began to believe that my behavior *dictated* how God responded to me. I had become, as monk Thomas Merton observed, "so obsessed" with the formulas and doing the formulas correctly that I "never [went] beyond the words to the ineffable reality which they attempt to convey."[1] The formulas had become the "ends in themselves" rather than the "means through which God communicates His truth."[2]

Rather than seeing formulas as one way—of many—to connect with God, formulas became The Way to Get God to Do What I Want. Tom Christofferson reached a similar realization in his own faith journey. He noted that he "had transformed the promise, 'I, the Lord, am bound when ye do what I say' (Doctrine and Covenants 82:10), into a sense that [his] righteousness could obligate Heavenly Father to do what [he] asked in the manner and timing that [he] wanted."[3]

I believed, however subtly, that by following a formula I could require God to respond to me in a certain way. This formulaic thinking did not seem harmful at first, because I was not asking for God to give me something material (money or a house or a job) or to interfere in another person's agency (such as changing someone's heart). I was just asking God to send me an answer to a gospel question. In my mind, that was a righteous desire that God should grant if I asked in a certain pre-calibrated way.

Yet the harm from this line of thinking is the idea that I could control anyone but myself. I had spent several years internalizing that I could only control myself. That concept was challenging for me, because I enjoy order and predictability and generally think that the world would run better if everyone did exactly as I told them to. But agency is foundational to our existence. The ability for each person to make his or her own choices and experience the natural consequences of those choices was one of God's first gifts to the human race. Lucifer wanted to supplant that gift with control and predictability. How often I favor Lucifer's plan in my life! How often I would rather control individuals outside of me—my family or my friends or my coworkers—rather than let them make their own choices and experience their own consequences.

I yearned for that control and predictability to extend to God. Wouldn't it be convenient if God had to respond in a particular way if I did certain things? In many ways, I liked the idea of a controllable god. A controllable god is a comfortable god. It is a predictable god who requires no risk from me. It is a god that I can reduce to lists and specific actions. It is a god I can craft into whatever image I want god to be.

Elder D. Todd Christofferson explained that "some misunderstand the promises of God to mean that obedience to Him yields specific outcomes on a fixed schedule."[4] This type of thinking turns God into a "cosmic vending machine where we (1) select a desired blessing, (2) insert the required sum of good works, and (3) the order is promptly delivered."[5] My desire for a controllable, transactional god turned God into a vending machine. I put the right amount of money into the machine, push the right buttons, and the thing I want pops out. The vending machine has no discretion. I ask and pay, and the vending machine gives. The vending machine is predictable, consistent, and completely responsive to all of my requests. If I want something from the machine, I get it.

But God's most compelling characteristics are incompatible with a vending-machine god.

For example, I am inspired by seeing the rulers of the universe as loving Heavenly Parents who are invested in me. Being given whatever I desire if I follow the right formula may seem like love, but it is not; it is just uncreative consistency. Pure love, as described in the scriptures, is patient and kind; it is not jealous, boastful, arrogant, rude, self-serving, or resentful (see 1 Corinthians 13:4–6).

Rather, it "bears all things, believes all things, hopes all things, and endures all things" (Wayment, 1 Corinthians 13:7). This love is more expansive, more risky, and more vulnerable than a simple I-ask/you-give type of relationship.

Sometimes true parental love is not giving a child what she wants; sometimes it is allowing a child some space to figure things out on her own. True love balances immediate desires with needed growth. Unfortunately, a vending-machine god cannot engage in that balance. And a *quid pro quo* relationship is not one borne of love but of economic advantage. I am drawn to a God who loves me, not one who is only interested in me solely because of the benefits I bring to the table. Thus, a vending-machine god is not one who embodies the loving involvedness I want to see in God.

I am also drawn to the notion that we are "joint heirs with Christ" (Romans 8:17). Those who receive God "receiveth my Father's kingdom; therefore all that my Father hath shall be given unto him" (Doctrine and Covenants 84:38). In the past, I pictured receiving the Father's kingdom like a Christmas present—something that is beautifully wrapped and fun to have. But the scriptures describe what God has as a "weight of glory" (2 Corinthians 4:17). God's responsibility and power is a weight, one which we must be prepared to shoulder. Strong backs do not come from sitting. Rather, strong backs come from working the muscles to the point that they tear slightly, and in the process of repairing those muscles, the body adds extra tissue to make the torn muscle stronger. If God always gives me what I want in a predictable way, I would never be forced to work hard enough to tear and then strengthen my emotional or spiritual muscles. And those strong muscles are necessary to handle the weight of glory that God wants to share.

I also am drawn to a God of grace. "When we talk about the grace of Jesus Christ," Sheri Dew writes, "we are talking about His power—power that enables us to do things we simply could not do on our own."[6] Grace is an enabling power that fills our lives and has nothing to do with our abilities or what we have done. Thus, as Emily Belle Freeman observes, "Grace is not about what *we* can do; it's all about what *He* can do."[7] And that grace has nothing to do with our abilities: "The Savior empowers us with His grace not because we've earned it, but because He loves us perfectly."[8] In fact, I love Adam Miller's idea that "God's creative work"—the creation of the world and the cosmos and us—"is the most fundamental expression of his grace, of his willingness to freely give what cannot be earned or deserved. . . . Grace is original. Grace is what comes first."[9] Grace is how God works.

But it is easy, when taking a more formulaic approach to the gospel, to avoid grace altogether, because if I have checked all the boxes, God has to respond to me in a certain way. This, Miller observed, is putting "God in *your* debt. Here, the more obedient I become, the less I figure I'll be indebted to God, the less grace I'll need, and the more in control I'll become."[10] But a controllable god, writes scholar Michael Austin, puts "God 'in moral bondage to the human race.' It destroys God's agency by setting up decision rules that determine how He must interact with His own creations."[11]

Thus, a vending-machine god limits God's power and ability to interact in my life. And a vending-machine god assumes that I know exactly what is best for me, that I have a global perspective on how my current actions will affect others or my future, and that I am the smartest one in the room. I have had enough life experience to know that these assumptions are incorrect.

The question, then, became what to put in place of the formulaic faith and a formulaic god. As I thought about this question, I was drawn to the story of Jesus raising Lazarus from the dead.

When Lazarus got sick, his sisters—Martha and Mary—sent word to Jesus about the illness. In that message they reminded Jesus that he loved Lazarus: "Lord, the one whom you love is ill" (Wayment, John 11:3). Jesus knew that the sickness would lead to Lazarus's death, but he said that Lazarus's sickness was "for the glory of God" (John 11:4). The scriptures mention that "Jesus loved Martha, and her sister, and Lazarus," but despite that love, Jesus "abode two days still in the same place where he was" (John 11:5–6). Jesus loved this family, but he did not immediately respond to their request. While Jesus waited, Lazarus's sickness took its natural course, and Lazarus died (see John 11:14). Only after Lazarus had been dead for four days did Jesus walk into Lazarus's town (see John 11:17).

Imagine how Martha felt as she sent for Jesus, hoped for his arrival, watched her brother die, and realized that Jesus had not come. She knew that Jesus had the power to heal Lazarus. In fact, Jesus had healed several people without even being in their presence or without being asked. He had healed the nobleman's son with just a few words: "Go, your son will live" (Wayment, John 4:50). Jesus never saw or touched the son; he just said those holy words to the father, and the son was healed at that moment. He healed a blind man and a man who had an infirmity for 38 years—neither of whom even *asked* to be healed (see John 5:5–8; 9:1–6). His healing, in some cases, was not contingent on people being aware of who he was or what he could do; he just healed because it helped those in need. Jesus had the power to heal from afar, and he had the disposition to heal those who did not even know he had that power. However, in the case of Lazarus—a man he loved from a family he loved—Jesus chose not to heal even when he was asked to do so.

From the perspective of a formulaic faith, this story does not compute. Even though Martha, Mary, and Lazarus lived righteously and asked properly, Jesus did not respond to them in the way that they had hoped; he had not prevented Lazarus from dying. Their righteous behavior did not require Jesus to respond to their request in a certain way; they were not in charge.

The scriptures do not reveal what went through Martha's mind while she waited for Jesus. But when Jesus did finally come, four days after Lazarus's death, the first statement Martha made to Jesus was a roundabout plea to resurrect Lazarus: "Lord, if you were here, my brother would not have died. But I know that even now if you ask God for something, God will give it to you" (Wayment, John 11:21–22). Rather than respond to her question, Jesus reaffirmed the general principle that all would be resurrected at some point—including Lazarus (see John 11:23–24). And then Jesus directed Martha to himself: "I am the resurrection and the life. Whoever believes in me, even if he is dead, will live. All who live and believe in me will never die. Do you believe this?" (Wayment, John 11:25–26). Even when Jesus came to Martha, he did not tell her that he would immediately resolve her greatest burden: her dead brother. He did not tell her that he would raise Lazarus from the dead; he did not tell her that all would be better. What he did do is point her to him and to the promises of eventual healing and life that he carried. And then he asked her if she believed.

Her answer to Jesus was yes, she still believed: "Yes, Lord. I believe that you are the Christ, the Son of God, the one who comes into the world" (Wayment, John 11:27). This was Martha's testimony. Despite Jesus not healing Lazarus or promising that he would resurrect Lazarus immediately, Martha believed that Jesus was God. She could believe even though Jesus had not shown up in her life as she had hoped. Her belief, then, was centered on Jesus and *who he was* and *what he had promised to do at some future point*, even though she did not have a timetable for when those promises would be fulfilled.

Jesus did eventually raise Lazarus from the dead. But Lazarus's resurrection was not the focus of the story: it was Martha's declaration of her faith in Jesus after a period of painful waiting. Perhaps that waiting space allowed Martha to wrestle with her belief and doubt in a way that an immediate healing would not. Perhaps there was something that Martha could learn from a space of waiting, hoping, and feeling disappointment that she could not learn if Jesus showed up promptly. And, importantly, her waiting space was not caused by divine neglect or disdain, nor was it triggered by the family's unrighteousness. Rather, all the scriptures mention about Jesus's decision to wait was that Lazarus's sickness was "for the glory of God" and that Jesus loved this family (John 11:4–5). Jesus's waiting was intentional and born from love and a broader perspective.

I am learning to be more like Martha: to found my faith on Jesus, not on formulas I expect Jesus to follow. Along these lines, Amy A. Wright, a counselor in the Primary General Presidency, wrote that "deliverance from our trials is different for each of us, and therefore our focus should be less about the *way* in which we are delivered and more about the Deliverer Himself."[12] My focus needs to be riveted on Jesus and *who he is* rather than *what I expect him to do.*

This can be really challenging, because innately I feel that if I am obedient then I should receive something in return. But I am learning that, as Adam Miller articulated, "the aim of the gospel isn't simply to give us what we think we want. Rather, its aim is to show us that what we thought we wanted isn't what God, in all his goodness and wisdom and mercy, is actually trying to give."[13] To that end, Terryl and Fiona Givens wrote that God's "divine energies are spent not in precluding chaos but in reordering it, not in preventing suffering but in alchemizing it, not in disallowing error but in transmuting it into goodness."[14] Sometimes that reordering, alchemizing, and transmuting occurs in spaces of weakness, disappointment, and quietness. Sometimes those are the only places where we are humble enough to see ourselves as we truly are and become willing to reach out to God as he truly is.

I am learning to base my faith on *just Jesus*. But sorting out *just Jesus* can be hard, because, as James Faulconer writes, "what we say about him is never more than a reflection of the particular circumstances in which we speak of him and the relationship that we have with him at that moment."[15] Perhaps we can have a clearer view of *just Jesus* if we examine our thoughts about Jesus and the motives underlying those thoughts. Do I talk about Jesus a certain way because it justifies my pride, my poor behavior, or my anger? Do I obey because I fear God? Or do I obey because I expect that God will be required to give me a blessing?

Carefully thinking about why I have taken a certain posture towards God has been a revealing experience, one that often shows me as immature and entitled. But perhaps that self-revelation is, in fact, a mark of Jesus working on my soul. As I begin to see myself as I truly am, I can begin to open my heart to Jesus.

All of this is not to say, however, that God does not keep promises. Oftentimes I have confused the promise-keeping God with the doing-certain-things-for-me-within-my-time-frame god. If God's actions fall outside my circumscribed ideas, then those actions—I have falsely reasoned—cannot be a fulfilment of his promises. But as Elder Jeffrey R. Holland counseled, "Sooner or later we learn that the times and seasons of our mortal journey are His and His alone to direct."[16] So "for every infirm man healed instantly as he waits to enter the Pool of Bethesda, someone else will spend 40 years in the desert waiting to enter the promised land. For every Nephi and Lehi divinely protected by an encircling flame of fire for their faith, we have an Abinadi burned at a stake of flaming fire for his."[17] Sometimes God does not show up when we want and how we want.

Just because God has not delivered us from our immediate distress does not mean that the work of deliverance is not going on deep within our souls. In my distress—when God felt very far away—I began to understand more deeply those who felt excluded and abandoned, and with that came greater compassion and kindness. I learned patience and gentleness with myself and others. I leaned into grace more than I ever had before. I had to choose these virtues rather than the magnetic pull of cynicism and nihilism.

And above all, I learned that control of anything or anybody but myself was a complete illusion. No matter how obedient I thought I was, my obedience could not control God. Our actions cannot "force our will upon God," President Dieter F. Uchtdorf wrote. "We cannot force God to comply with our desires—no matter how right we think we are or how sincerely we pray."[18] My obedience did not require God to respond to me in a particular way. I had to let God be God. Letting go of timing and a notion that God had to perform in a certain way released my perceived control of God and allowed me to embrace a loving, grace-filled Being who wanted me to grow to the point that I could bear an eternal weight of glory with him.

Faith, Rethought

As I rethought quietness and a formulaic God, I reached a point where I needed to rethink faith.

I used to think of faith as something that just happened to me, something that was external to myself. In many ways, I saw faith as a cloud that would rest on people and they would "have faith." But a few years ago, I realized that faith arose from thoughts I had about God. That made faith in God not something external that happened to me. Rather, faith became more of a choice: I could choose the thoughts I had about God, and I could choose thoughts that engendered trust in God.

This worked well for me until I hit the wall of divine quietness. Many of the thoughts I had about God seemed to be untrue in light of what I was experiencing. Without those anchoring thoughts, my trust in God evaporated. I believed that I could choose thoughts that would create trust in God, but I was not sure what those thoughts were or if I even wanted them. For some time, faith seemed like a choice that was unavailable to me.

With faith and belief seeming too far away to grasp, I latched onto the concept of desire: I could desire to have faith, I could desire to believe, even if I did not feel like I could have faith or believe at the moment. I took solace in President Dieter F. Uchtdorf's teaching that desire is "enough to start."[1] As President Russell M. Nelson taught, "Exercising faith can seem overwhelming. At times we may wonder if we can possibly muster enough faith to receive the blessings that we so desperately need. However, the Lord put those fears to rest through the words of the Book of Mormon prophet Alma. Alma asks us simply to *experiment* upon the word and 'exercise a *particle* of faith, yea, even if [we] can no more than desire to believe' [Alma 32:27]."[2] Desire is the foundation. That is because, as President Dallin H. Oaks taught, "Desires dictate our priorities, priorities shape our choices, and choices determine our actions. The desires we act on determine our changing, our achieving, and our becoming."[3] Thus, "what we insistently desire, over time," Elder Neal A. Maxwell wrote, "is what we will eventually become and what we will receive in eternity."[4]

A desire is something that we long for, even if we do not think it is likely to be attained. Although I felt for some time that merely desiring God was a sign of God's absence, I loved the idea that desiring and longing for God "is possible only through God's own hidden presence. We cannot long for something that is not intimately close to us. Thirst is more than absence of water. It is not experienced by stones, but only by living beings that depend on water. Who knows more about living water, the person who opens the water tap daily without much thinking, or the thirst tortured traveler in the desert in search for a spring?"[5] I felt a longing for God, even if sometimes I felt that God did not long for me.

Regardless of how I felt at some of my lowest points, I could not deny that at times in my life I had palpably felt that God knew who I was and cared for me. In fact, about one month or so into this quietness, I went to the temple to find some relief. I did an initiatory session. During the initiatory ceremony, a temple worker stopped what she was saying, put her hands on my face, and said, "You are so precious." She looked me in the eyes and then continued with the ceremony. For a moment, I realized that God knew who I was, even though the heavens were quiet and I was struggling with liking God.

I held onto that and a few other experiences where I had felt the Spirit strongly. I remembered feeling an overwhelming warmth when I was given the gift of the Holy Ghost when I was eight years old. I remembered sitting with my mother at a fireside when I was a teenager, and together we sang "I Believe in Christ." That day, that song spoke to my soul, and I felt strongly that I actually did believe. I remembered beautiful testimony meetings during girls' camps and youth conferences; I remembered reading the scriptures and feeling fire in my heart. And I remembered sitting in an endowment session one year prior to the quietness and feeling an unexplainable and unexpected love for every person in the room, none of whom I knew.

Remembering these events as instances where I had felt God's love and influence gave enough fuel to my desire to keep it flickering. Although at my lowest points I wanted to look back at my life and see an absent God, remembering these events pushed me to question that interpretation of my history. When I chose to remember an event in my life as evidence of a God who at the very least cared about me, my desire to stay with God grew.

This small desire worked on me slowly, over a period of several months. That desire grew gently into belief. As I started managing my anxiety and depression, challenging my unhelpful thoughts about quietness, and questioning my thoughts about a formulaic god, I again began to believe that God was loving. I started to believe that it was possible that a loving, intentional God could go quiet for good reason. I began to engage with my doubts—rather than succumbing to them—and with that engagement came the beginnings of a belief that quietness could do something to my soul that talkativeness could not.

Elder Jeffrey R. Holland has taught that "*belief* is a precious word, an even more precious act," and we "need never apologize for 'only believing.'"[6] For several months, I was in this "only believing" space. On one hand, it felt fantastic to be in a spot where I could choose to believe—where I could choose to think thoughts about God that were helpful and uplifting rather than harmful. But on the other hand, I felt the pull to work towards faith.

I had never really thought about the difference between belief and faith. But Brian McLaren articulated his distinction between the two, and I found his description compelling: "The believer will open his mind to the truth on the condition that it fits in with his preconceived ideas and wishes. Faith, on the other hand, is an unreserved opening of the mind to the truth, whatever it may turn out to be. Faith has no preconceptions; it is a plunge into the unknown. Belief clings, but faith lets go."[7] To illustrate this point, he notes that "faith is like looking at the sky through a clear or open window . . . with an openness to accepting it as it is: blue or gray, light or dark, starry or sunny, rainy or fair. But beliefs are like blue paint that people decide to apply to the window glass to be sure it will always be the color they wish it to be."[8]

Faith, then, requires more of me than belief, because it requires more than "intellectual assent to a set of doctrines."[9] It requires that I have confidence in and rely on what (or Who) I believe. In other words, faith can be a synonym for trust.[10] I found myself in a space where I could believe in God, but I did not trust God.

Choosing faith was difficult because, fundamentally, I still struggled with wanting a formulaic god; I wanted to know that if I did certain things, God would respond in a particular way. It was easier to trust a God that I could predict and control rather than a God who was an agent to himself, who could choose to interact in my life however he pleased.

I had to get comfortable with being uncomfortable. I needed to let go of the idea that I could know enough about God to predict his movements in my life. I had to learn to trust him, even though I could not predict his movements.

The scriptures consistently invite us to seek to know God. But that certainly does not mean that God, as a whole, can be completely knowable. For example, Isaiah tells us to "seek ye the Lord while he may be found, call ye upon him while he is near" (Isaiah 55:6). He encourages us to forsake our ways and our thoughts and "return unto the Lord" (Isaiah 55:7). Yet following the invitation to come to know God is a reminder that there is mystery to God that our minds cannot understand: "For my thoughts are not your thoughts, neither are your ways my ways, saith the Lord. For as the heavens are higher than the earth, so are my ways higher than your ways, and my thoughts than your thoughts" (Isaiah 55:8–9).

Similarly, Jacob tells us that "it is impossible that man should find out all [God's] ways" (Jacob 4:8). But that doesn't mean that all of God is off the table. Rather, Jacob emphasizes that "no man knoweth of his ways save it be revealed unto him" (Jacob 4:8). God reveals *some* of his ways. And how and when he reveals his ways is "in his own time, and in his own way, and according to his own will" (Doctrine and Covenants 88:68).

When God does reveal himself, sometimes the gap between God and humans is even more profound. For example, after Moses spoke with God face-to-face, he said, "Now, for this cause I know that man is nothing, which thing I never had supposed" (Moses 1:10). Since there is a gap between God and me and I can only know God's ways through revelation given at God's will, the likelihood of me completely understanding the contours of God and how God will react in certain situations is nonexistent. If my trust was predicated on predicting God, then I would never trust God.

It turns out that most people—me included—prefer "the definitive" and have "discomfort with ambiguity."[11] In discussing ambiguity, Brigham Young University professor Anthony Sweat summarized a series of studies where researchers examined individuals' abilities to cope with ambiguity. Those studies found that "those with low tolerance for ambiguity tend to solve problems without adequate information."[12] In relating these studies to some church members' resistance to ambiguity, he noted, "Some Saints are willing to swallow convenient doctrinal pills that allow us merely to sleep well at night. Revelation, however, often requires sleepless nights and jolts us from ambiguous dreams (see Genesis 37). It asks for seekers to go forward, not clearly knowing what the Lord intends or plans (see 1 Nephi 4:6). Church members who just want to rest easy are not truth seekers; rather they are comfort seekers."[13]

Sweat emphasized the necessity of getting comfortable with ambiguity: "True seekers understand that, of necessity, ambiguity and gray areas exist, and they embrace rather than fear the inherent uncertainties. The possibilities fascinate them rather than threatening the veneer of peace that the overly definitive creates. It is the very acknowledgment of uncertainties that causes true seekers to look at subtleties, new angles, and potential alternatives and to be open to new ideas, often leading to further light and truth. Embracing ambiguity, ironically, can eventually lead to clearer answers in the end than the comfortable, dogmatic declarative. *Ambiguity can be one of the best friends of faith.*"[14] My faith can be strengthened by my willingness to be comfortable with ambiguity and uncertainty.

I am also learning that I can have faith in a God who occasionally disappoints me. I had an idea that God could not disappoint me because God is perfect. I had several ideas that resided in absolutes about how God would *always* show up in my life and therefore *always* meet my expectations. But my expectations are limited by my view; they are not divine and sometimes not even in my best interests. A perfect God should not be confined to meeting my expectations, because my expectations are not perfect. Disappointment is a natural part of a life of faith in a Being that I do not completely understand or control.

Jesus's last hours are an example of willingness to experience disappointment while still holding onto faith. As Wendy Ulrich wrote, "In Gethsemane, although He has taught His disciples that God knows how to give good gifts to His children and will not, if they ask for bread or fish, give them a stone or a serpent, Jesus's petition for the removal of the bitter cup is not granted."[15] Even though God did not remove the bitter cup from Jesus, God did send "an angel unto him from heaven, strengthening him" (Luke 22:43). Jesus did receive some divine help. But on Calvary, Jesus's "question about God's apparent absence goes unanswered."[16] Thus,

"Gethsemane required Jesus to accept the strengthening hand of a messenger—instead of the escape He had prayed for. Calvary required Jesus to hold fast to what He knew about His Father's love—even when His Father seemed far away."[17] Jesus could trust in God in all circumstances, including when it would have been easy to conclude that God was absent or aloof.

Learning to trust in God—and in trusting, to embrace uncertainty and vulnerability—is my work to do. In fact, I wondered for several months what I would base my faith on if I did not base my faith on formulas. What does that look like? How could I trust in a God who was not responsive when I asked and who may not be responsive in the future? A set of authors suggested that instead of grounding faith in an obedience-reward system, we should ground our faith "in the goodness of God."[18] I wondered what that meant or how that felt. Then one day, my son showed me a video he had seen in school, a video of random individuals helping each other. In that unexpected space, I was overwhelmed with the feeling that God was good. I finally began to understand the concept that goodness comes from somewhere, and that somewhere is God. I am learning that it is possible to base my faith on the goodness of God: Jesus is good.

My faith is small. That is okay. All I need is faith like a mustard seed, something that is small but has the potential for great growth. Now, as I am learning to be more flexible in my thinking, more willing to embrace ambiguity, and more willing to risk vulnerability, I am creating room for my faith to truly grow.

Spiritual Nourishment

While I struggled with my faith, the things that used to bring a sense of closeness with God—such as prayer and scripture study—no longer worked. Not only did they feel hollow, but sometimes they were painful. They were reminders of the faith and closeness I once felt. They highlighted my distance from God and what I lacked.

For years, I had cultivated an interest in scripture study. But in divine quietness, when I opened the scriptures all I saw was a wrathful God. On the other hand, I had never been particularly good at prayer. I have sat in rooms with those who seem to pray to a God who is immediately present; I never figured out how to achieve that type of closeness. Yet prayer was still part of my routine, and once in a while I would feel a brief connection. In quietness, however, much of my desire to pray disappeared. The prayers I did say were not earnest. I was trying to get rid of a formulaic version of God, and I wasn't sure how that translated into prayer. Should I ask for anything at all?

I appreciated the writing of Terryl and Fiona Givens about finding spiritual nourishment when in a place of doubt: "Spiritual strength requires finding one's own well from which to drink. We should recognize, first, that we are responsible for our own

SPIRITUAL NOURISHMENT

spiritual diet, and second, that sources of inspiration are sprinkled indiscriminately throughout time and place."[1] Even in a place of doubt, I needed to take responsibility for feeding my spirit. How could I navigate a space where certain spiritual practices were currently unfulfilling or hurtful but had the potential to stimulate growth or connectedness at some future point? I needed to find something that would feed my spirit in my present place.

That meant I plodded through the tried-and-true spiritual practices—although they did not feel inspiring or uplifting—while searching for things that fed my soul. Most of my spiritual nourishment came in books from a variety of religious traditions and in conversations with those who were also struggling with their faith. Other faith traditions' writings on doubt, divine quietness, and scripture brought comfort and a renewed interest to reengage in scripture and prayer. Speaking with others about how they were navigating their faith struggles while moving forward in the church gave me courage to continue trying.

To breathe life back into those simple spiritual practices, I needed to look at them more broadly and with more openness and curiosity. Rather than treating spiritual practices as a set of easy answers, checklists, and simple to-dos, spiritual practices became more expansive: I expanded what "counted" as a spiritual practice. I spent much more time hiking in nature, walking with friends, digging in the dirt, and sitting in quiet spaces. Writing this book was a spiritual practice.

I also expanded how I thought about scripture study and prayer—the more traditional spiritual practices—and my heart and minded expanded in turn.

SCRIPTURE STUDY

A few months after the quietness started, I was determined to figure out who God was by reading all the standard works with the question *Who is God?* in mind.

I first opened the Old Testament. Genesis gave hope—I saw God showing up in messed-up families and in the wilderness, and I saw him speaking directly to women. This was a good start. Then I hit Exodus, and the chapters on the tabernacle were not that inspiring. Leviticus felt like a terribly long list of everything that I could do wrong, and I envisioned God sitting in heaven giving out demerits for every wrong step. And it went downhill from there. There were lots of commandments, not a lot of love, and so much gratuitous violence and war in God's name. I almost slammed the book shut when I read in Judges 19 about a Levite cutting his concubine into twelve pieces and sending those pieces to all the coasts of Israel. But it was David that pushed me over the edge. His life was a soap opera, so violence-filled, and it just kept going and going. I gave up in Chronicles. I thought either the God portrayed in the Old Testament was terrible and not worth my time, or the Old Testament simply does not point to God.

The New Testament was a little better. In the gospels, Jesus reached out to the forgotten and abused. He had beautiful teachings about love—yet some of his sayings were harsh. And the epistles mentioned God's wrath with frequency. When I dipped into the Book of Mormon and the Doctrine and Covenants, I kept seeing an angry God, a demanding God, and an insensitive God. In my quietness, the scriptures reminded me of God's anger rather than his love.

Two years later, the scriptures became a place of growth and learning. Rather than walking away from challenging passages with a distaste for God, I saw those passages as an invitation to think more deeply. I saw God showing up in unexpected places and in unexpected ways. The people in the scriptures were flawed but redeemable. In other words, the scriptures became less of a place of injury and more of a place of wrestling. I was getting to the point where I could answer yes to Sheri Dew's question: "Are you willing to engage in the wrestle? In an ongoing spiritual wrestle?"[2]

A few things helped me get there.

First was the realization that scriptures act as a mirror: what we learn from them can be more a reflection of ourselves at that moment than a reflection of God. I was hurt because God went quiet. Although I wanted to find God in the scriptures, I was angry, and I thought that God was unkind, demanding, and wrathful because he went quiet. And those insecurities and fears came through in my scripture reading. I saw what I was looking for.

That can be true for almost any principle. I can find support in the scriptures for a loving God. Some passages promote forgiveness. Others hammer judgment. Some emphasize mercy and grace. Others focus on works. Some justify violence. Others advocate for peace.

Because of the diversity in scripture, it was important for me to be aware of my mindset when I was reading. I was going to find whatever I was looking for.

Second, I learned that the diversity in scripture is informative for our faith. Oftentimes the diversity in scripture can cause confusion. This is nothing new. When Joseph Smith was wrestling with which church to join, he noted, "The teachers of religion of the different sects understood the same passages of scripture so differently as to destroy all confidence in settling the question by an appeal to the Bible" (Joseph Smith–History 1:12). The scriptures, rather than settling questions, sometimes just make more of them.

Elder Lynn G. Robbins has articulated one reason why the scriptures may seem to point in opposite directions. He reasoned, "Many gospel principles come in pairs, meaning one is incomplete without the other."[3] Some pairs include agency and responsibility, mercy and justice, faith and works, and grace and obedience.

These complementary principles need each other. For example, if we focus only on grace, then we forget God's commandments. But the commandments allow us to live a life that is trustworthy and closer to the life that God lives. If we truly want to become like God, we need to follow the path—including the commandments—that he has set out for us. On the other hand, if we focus only on commandments and forget grace, we end up with toxic perfectionism. In many ways, we write Jesus out of our lives, removing God's help because we strain to follow every iota of every commandment. Complementary principles prevent us from leaning too far on one side or the other. They ask that we find a balance between the two.

Finding balance, however, often requires some discomfort and frequent recalibrating. It is far easier to rest on one side of a complementary principle. I have to do far fewer mental gymnastics if I, for example, view my life through the lens of justice. I can mete out judgment to anyone who is not following the commandments perfectly. I can judge myself; I can confidently say how God will judge others. Things get more complicated, however, if I need to discern the wiser choice—justice or mercy or a combination of the two—in any given situation. That requires me to push against knee-jerk reactions and really think deeply about my role, God's wisdom, the agency of others, and the interaction of other gospel principles. Balance requires more work.

Balance pushes us out of the all-or-nothing mindset and towards a *both-and* mindset. Interestingly, all-or-nothing thinking is a common cognitive distortion in those who are depressed. All-or-nothing thinking places us in extremes: either I am perfect or a failure; either school is worth my time or it's a complete waste; either my friend is thoughtful or horrible; either my work is inspiring or drudgery. There is no middle ground. But reality is often found in the middle ground.

In my case, my cognitive distortion about God was that either he was loving and therefore always responsive *or* he was angry and therefore unresponsive. This left no middle ground. Moving towards a both-and mindset—a mindset that saw complementary principles—allowed me to consider that God could be both loving and unresponsive, or loving and also angry at times. God could be both. A God that created complementary principles was probably also a God that embodied complementary attributes.

Third, diversity in the scriptures also builds faith because it portrays a variety of approaches to faith and faith experiences. For example, Bible scholar Peter Enns writes about the three general categories of Psalms in the Bible: "1. Everything is fine. God is great. Stay the course. 2. Things are terribly wrong, and I am at the end of my rope, but thank you Lord for coming to my rescue (alternate ending: I know you'll come to my rescue soon/eventually). 3. Things are terribly wrong, I am at the end of my rope, and to make things worse, Oh Lord, you're nowhere to be found."[4]

For an example of the God-is-gone category, he points to Psalm 88, where the Psalmist writes that he has "cried day and night" before God, but God has "laid me in the lowest pit, in darkness, in the deeps" (Psalm 88:1, 6). The Psalmist continues, "Lord, why castest thou off my soul? why hidest thou thy face from me?" (Psalm 88:14). Enns notes that feeling that God is gone is "never judged, shamed, or criticized by God. Worshipping other gods or acting unjustly toward others gets criticized about every three sentences, but not this honest talk of feeling abandoned by God."[5] He argues that scriptures like these "relay the experiences of ancient men and women of *faith*, and were kept because those experiences were common—*part of being an Israelite and therefore valued*. For us they signal not only what *can* happen in the life of faith, but also what *does* happen—what we should *expect* to happen."[6]

Our scriptures—especially the Bible—were written and edited by dozens and dozens of individuals, all coming from different backgrounds and faith perspectives. These multiple perspectives do not reduce the authority of scripture; rather, they give the scriptures more richness. They allow individuals at varying parts of their faith journey to find hope. Frankly, in my darkest moments, I needed Psalm 88 as a reminder that quietness happens to lots of faithful people and is painful.

I can read the scriptures now and look at the writers and the actors as examples of a variety of faith journeys and approaches to God. As Rachel Held Evans wrote, "God gave us a cacophony of voices and perspectives, all in conversation with one another, representing the breadth and depth of the human experience in all its complexities and contradictions."[7] These scriptural writings "avoid simplistic solutions to complex problems. It's almost as though God trusts us to approach [those problems] with wisdom, to use discernment as we read and interpret, and to remain open to other points of view."[8]

Fourth, it has been helpful to recognize that the language used in the scriptures is a human's interpretation of a revelation from God; the "*records of such revelations are not the revelations themselves.*"[9] Rather, all scripture is "limited by mortal constraints,"[10] such as culture, opinions, perspective, memory, and language.[11] The scriptures, then, are not meant "to be a perfect record of God's dialect or diction but to act as a personal Urim and Thummim—a launchpad for revelation to connect us to the same divine source that revealed the truths in the first place."[12] President Dallin H. Oaks repeated the same refrain: "For us, the scriptures are not the ultimate source of knowledge, but what precedes the ultimate source. The ultimate knowledge comes by revelation."[13]

Along these lines, Fiona and Terryl Givens have advocated approaching "scriptural reading in the light of core Restoration teachings that advise us to be cautious in our assumptions about scriptural inerrancy."[14] According to them, "recognizing that the scriptures are fallible—and that superficial readings are harmful—gives us liberty to approach the scriptures with caution and with a more questing spirit."[15]

The scriptures are, quite frankly, humanity's best shot at articulating God's inspiration. That inspiration can be hard to express in words, especially if that inspiration comes in a feeling or a sense that something is true or involves something that is not within our daily experience. Recognizing this, I can give the writers of the scriptures grace: they did their best with what they had. As I approach the scriptures willing to give the writers grace, hopefully the ensuing openness and curiosity will allow me to have insights into the scriptures that I never had before.

Along with giving the scripture writers grace, I can examine their articulation of certain principles through the lens of the restored gospel. For example, I was troubled by the violence I saw in the Old Testament, especially since so much of it was attributed to God. But as I thought about this violence, Doctrine and Covenants 98 came to mind. In that section, God discusses violence and self-defense. He encourages the Saints to bear violence against them patiently (see Doctrine and Covenants 98:23–27). God states that at some point, the Saints are justified in using violence, but that if they abstain from violence, they will be "rewarded for [their] righteousness" (Doctrine and Covenants 98:30). This modern-day revelation allowed me to ponder about the violence in the Old Testament, and whether it was justified or directed by God.

Fifth, in the process of broadening my understanding of the scriptures, I have adopted President Russell M. Nelson's mantra, "Good inspiration is based upon good information."[16] The scriptures were all written in cultures that no longer exist; some of those cultures are thousands of years old. Our translations and publications of the scriptures are old, too. The King James Bible was published in 1611; that is about the time that William Shakespeare was writing. Whenever I read Shakespeare, I purchase an edition with Shakespeare's writing on one page and notes on the adjacent page—because without those notes, I miss or misunderstand good chunks of what Shakespeare is saying. The same applies to our Bible. Because the language of the King James Version is old—but beautiful—I sometimes misunderstand the meaning of the words. My understanding of the Bible has been enhanced by good study Bibles, a concordance, other versions of the Bible, and reading from those who have spent their lives studying the Bible. These have given me more space to think about complementary principles, how God works through flawed individuals, and how God shows up in unexpected places.

The same applies to the Book of Mormon, the Doctrine and Covenants, and the Pearl of Great Price. Better understanding the Bible enhances study of the Book of Mormon and the Pearl of Great Price, since both of those scriptures involve cultures that were born from the Bible. And the Doctrine and Covenants becomes more applicable when I understand the context of the revelations—what was happening in Joseph Smith's life at the time he received the revelation. For example, Elder Dale G. Renlund recounted that when he became the advisor over the Church History Department, he read all the volumes of The Joseph Smith Papers. For him, "reading everything Joseph Smith ever wrote or was reported to have said has simply strengthened [his] testimony of [Joseph's] role as a prophet chosen of God to restore His work on earth."[17] More information about the scriptures creates a larger reservoir that both the Spirit and I can draw from as I am wrestling with them.

Finally, I am learning to approach the scriptures with more curiosity. I try not to make quick decisions about what a scripture means. I am working on keeping my mind open to many reasons why a passage may be phrased in a particular way. It is an interesting balance—paying attention to specific words and phrases while simultaneously acknowledging that since the scriptures are very much a divine project filtered through humans, the choice of words and phrases may not carry as much weight as I thought.

The scriptures have become an invitation to wrestle with God. In that wrestling, Lauren Winner has written that when a phrase of scripture "rubs you the wrong way but you find yourself unable to set down the rankling thing and move on, the rankling might in fact be the Holy Spirit's way of getting your attention, of fixing your eyes and asking you to look more closely at the prayer or parable or painting or phrase—to discover what it holds for you, if only you'd be willing to explore it, and yourself, deeply enough."[18] She asserts that when she reads difficult scriptural passages, she resists the impulse to ignore them or throw them out. Rather, she writes, "Those passages are there, in the scriptures, [and] since this is the Word of God, we are committed to wrestling with it, in the belief that it will eventually bless us, even if we come away from the wrestling limping, like Jacob."[19]

I can only wrestle with the scriptures if I am willing to engage with them, even with the most challenging passages. If I choose not to engage, I learn nothing.

At this point, some days my scripture study feels exciting, and other days it feels uninspiring. Sometimes I am just slogging through, without feeling much in return. But that simply means that scripture study is no different than any other endeavor in my life. Whether it is school, work, family, or hobbies, sometimes the work is exciting, and sometimes it's drudgery. But I show up because the work is important. Showing God that I am willing to engage in his words for a short time each day is a little thing that compounds over time. It is a way for me to remember God, even if that remembering lasts a few short minutes. And it allows me to continue the practice of openness and curiosity.

PRAYER

Because I connected my quietness with unanswered prayers, I was cautious with my approach to prayer. I struggled with feeling that my prayers weren't going anywhere. I feared asking questions. What if they were not answered again? Could I handle more quietness? If I did not ask questions or ask for help, then maybe I would be leaving blessings on the table. If I prayed and was okay with not getting an answer, did that mean I was not praying with enough faith? Did that then mean that I would not get an answer?

I don't yet have good answers for these questions. Praying is a practice that takes a lifetime of effort. But I realized that my approach to prayer was too narrow, in that I only considered things as "prayers" if they opened with "Heavenly Father," gave thanks, asked for blessings, and ended with "in the name of Jesus Christ, amen." Certainly this form of prayer is important; it is the form of prayer that Jesus taught his disciples. But if prayer is "first and foremost a vehicle of relationship,"[20] then prayer can look like a lot of things. It can look like the Lord's Prayer. It can be talking out loud while kneeling, whispering while lying down, pouring out thoughts while walking. It can be telling God about our day, our hopes, and our dreams. It can be inviting God into a still space or into a working space. It can be pondering on a scripture.

Monk Thomas Merton wrote that it is "the will to pray that is the essence of prayer, and the desire to find God, to see Him and to love Him is the one thing that matters."[21] He encouraged praying "by peaceful, even perhaps inarticulate, efforts to center your heart upon God, Who is present to you in spite of all that may be going through your mind."[22]

Along these lines, a group of therapists who are also members of the church encouraged members to "consider approaching some prayers as one would sitting by a warm fire with a beloved friend—not with a wordy agenda, but with full presence and appreciation."[23] To do that, we have to cultivate a "'loving awareness of the presence of God'" and consent to God's action in our lives, whatever that looks like.[24] And to fully consent to God's presence and action in our lives, we may need to empty ourselves—"our minds, our stories, our expectations of what 'should' be happening—in order for us to be taught and tutored by Him."[25]

I was particularly moved by a story I read about a woman who was overwhelmed with her life responsibilities and was ashamed that she was not doing all the church things she should be doing—such as attending the temple, holding family home evening, or consistently praying.[26] She decided that she wanted to change her relationship with God, but she wanted that change to be something small and sustainable. So she decided that she would sit for fifteen minutes twice each week and invite God to sit with her. She found that sitting for fifteen minutes was more challenging than she initially thought, because she was "deeply afraid that, if given the chance, God would just add a big bunch of stuff to *The List* and then walk away, going back to His very important life and leaving her to manage alone."[27] But as she prioritized sitting twice each week, she began to feel that God did come sit with her, and when he did, he did not bring a list of things for her to do.

One day as she sat, she brought her long to-do list with her. She looked it over and asked God where to begin. "She felt the answer, slow and gentle, 'These are all good things. You can do whatever you like. But this is not what I care about right now. I care about you.'"[28] Several weeks into the sitting, she heard the answer, "'There *is* something I'd like you to work on: Enjoy your children.'"[29]

Wendy Ulrich, who recounted this woman's story, emphasized that when this woman "made the time to sit patiently through her resistance, fear, and sorrow and invited God to sit with her, He came. And He came with only love, not a list, in His hand. . . . She still finds it hard to take the time to sit still, or to tolerate the closeness she both longs for and fears with a God she still doesn't completely trust to be on her side. But God still comes and sits, often, and He still waits patiently for her when she waits for Him."[30]

I am finding that, like this woman, I feel resistance to God. I fear what I will find if I look too closely, or if I allow God to get too close to me. So often I cover these fears with words, with prayers about my standard set of worries—family, friends, and work. But sitting in silence and inviting God to join me is a different kind of prayer; for me, that requires more vulnerability. It is a harder prayer. Ulrich notes that we can engage in this kind of prayer by "simply invit[ing] God to join us at whatever empty chair we see or can imagine, opening our heart to let Him come close and sit with us as we wrestle with a problem, or feel sad, or just stare in wonder at the night sky."[31] This is a type of prayer I had never thought about before.

Another type of prayer that struck me was one that springs from pondering scripture. This type of praying is called Ignatian prayer, which is "about hearing God speak to you through the scriptures. You pick a passage of scripture . . . and, using all your senses, you imagine the story and the scene. . . . Imagine yourself in the story; allow yourself to encounter the place and to encounter

God in that place, and see what God has for you, in that place, in that story."[32]

When I read about Ignatian prayer, I decided to give it a try with where I was in the scriptures. I was in Doctrine and Covenants 30—a section of scripture that is devoted at first to the Lord correcting David Whitmer. The first verse reads: "Behold, I say unto you, David, that you have feared man and have not relied on me for strength as you ought" (Doctrine and Covenants 30:1). I pictured in my mind the scene: this revelation was received in September 1830. Earlier that year, Joseph Smith had published the Book of Mormon and formally established the church. Church members had faced increased persecution over the summer months, with groups of angry townsfolk destroying dams that created pools in a river deep enough for prospective members to be baptized. Hiram Page, one of the eight witnesses to the Book of Mormon, had seemingly received instructions through a seer stone that contradicted some of the things that Joseph Smith had preached. At this time of internal and external distress, Joseph was also thinking about how to spread the gospel message through missionary work, something that would strain the little congregation even more.[33]

I thought about all these circumstances and imagined how David Whitmer might have felt. Maybe he thought that because he believed he was in God's church, things would be easier. Maybe he was disappointed in Joseph's leadership. Maybe he was anxious for his future. Maybe, as one of the three witnesses to the Book of Mormon—privileged with only a few others to see the plates—he was feeling a dearth of the spiritual ecstasy that followed that experience.

I put myself in his shoes, imagining an itchy collar and a hot jacket. I imagined the weather in New England in September: cool, with a light breeze, and the leaves beginning to change. I pictured Joseph dictating a few short words of that revelation and David's brother writing them down. I imagined if I had read those words, I would have felt hot-cheeked and embarrassed. And I would have been at a little bit of a loss about how to respond.

Then I pictured those words being aimed at me. Was it possible that I had "feared man" more than God and had not relied on God for strength as I should have? In my struggles with God, was it possible that I had leaned away from God's words a bit and relied on others and myself for strength? What did relying on God's strength mean in this scenario?

While I pondered what it meant to rely on God's strength, a comment came to mind that I had heard in a church meeting: a member had talked about how she had tried to lay her burdens at Jesus's feet. Perhaps giving Jesus our burdens is one way of relying on God's strength. So I pictured myself carrying my burdens in some sort of bundle and walking up some stairs. At the top of the stairs was Jesus. I could not picture his face, but I could picture his arms. I visualized giving my bundle to him, and he took it and cared for it. That Ignatian prayer was a gift.

While exploring different kinds of prayer, I remind myself that questions are good, even though it was questioning that got me into this mess. Growth and revelation come from questioning; stagnation comes when we do not ask. Along these lines, Sheri Dew wrote, "Asking inspired questions leads to knowledge. It leads to revelation. It leads to greater faith. And it leads to peace. Not asking questions, on the other hand, closes off revelation, growth, learning, progression, and the ministering of the Holy Ghost."[34]

And Rachel Held Evans noted, "Serious doubt, the kind that leads to despair, does not begin when we start asking God questions, but when out of fear, we stop."[35]

In the scriptures, God's responses to questions have been varied. Sometimes he answers with a miraculous vision, as he did with Joseph Smith's First Vision. Sometimes he responds to direct questions, such as when Ammon asked God if the Anti-Nephi-Lehies should leave Lamanite lands, and God said yes (see Alma 27:7–12). Other times, God does not answer the question, but he gives something else instead. For example, when Jacob was wrestling God, God gave him the name Israel (see Genesis 32:28). After God gave Jacob that name, Jacob asked God a question: "Tell me, I pray thee, thy name" (Genesis 32:29). God refused to answer Jacob's question and instead blessed Jacob (see Genesis 32:29). Perhaps God's varied answers to questions are a way that "all things work together for good to them that love God" (Romans 8:28).

Spiritual nourishment, through a time of quietness, required broadening and stretching. I had to recognize how my thinking patterns affected my scripture study. I had to reach for resources that I had never before considered. And I had to learn to engage with the scriptures, even with passages that I did not like. As for prayer, I learned to broaden my definition of prayer, focusing on my intent in praying rather than on rigid form. I learned to hold an intention to connect with God in any way that I could, and I am trying to be open to the many ways he could present himself. Finding forms of scripture study and prayer that resonated with me brought these practices back to life in a form that was richer than before.

The Body of Christ

Quietness gave me space to rethink my spiritual practices. When I was having a hard time liking God—when I was unsure whether I wanted to stay with God—church was a hard place to be. The certainty some have about God can be grating at times. I often felt that I did not belong. A few times my heart hurt more walking out of the chapel than it did when I walked in. Let me be clear: When I shared my struggles with members of my congregation, I felt nothing but love and compassion and confidence that I could get through it. But church was still a hard place to be because my experience felt very different from what I heard from the pulpit.

Although church was hard for me at times, I found power in meeting with those who are trying. Zion is a community project, not an individual one. Zion requires people who have "one heart and one mind" (Moses 7:18). This does not mean that everyone turns into a same-thinking robot. Rather, having one heart and one mind, as Elder D. Todd Christofferson put it, means that God's "will and interest [become] our greatest desire."[1] "Commitment is the key, not a lack of disagreement," wrote Anthony Sweat. "Unity is based on solidarity, not homogeneity in thought."[2]

The best scriptural example of unity among diverse members

is Paul's comparison of the church to the body of Christ. Paul talks about the members being "one body" because they are "all baptized into one body in one Spirit" (Wayment, 1 Corinthians 12:12–13). Although the members are part of one body, they are all different. There are feet and hands and ears and eyes and noses. And they are all important: "If the whole body were an eye, how would the body hear? If the whole body were an ear, how would the body have a sense of smell? . . . If all were one member, where would the body be?" (Wayment, 1 Corinthians 12:17, 19). "The eye cannot say to the hand, 'I have no need of you,' nor can the hand say to the feet, 'I have no need of you.' Instead, the members of the body, even though they seem to be weaker, are essential, and those members of the body that seem less honorable, we place greater honor on them, and our unpresentable body parts are clothed with greater respect, which our more presentable parts do not need" (Wayment, 1 Corinthians 12:21–24). Paul concludes: "God has brought the body together. . . . You are the body of Christ, and each member has a part" (Wayment, 1 Corinthians 12:24, 27).

Each member of the church is different. But those differences *strengthen* the entire body of the church. Paul recognizes that the body works best when its various parts are healthy and when those parts are not trying to be something that they are not. For example, the body works best when the eye operates as an eye and is not trying to be a foot, or when the foot works as a foot and is not trying to be the pancreas. Each part is valuable in its own right, and each part does the most good to the body when it lives up to its own uniqueness.

Being fully a foot—or an eye or a nose or a pancreas—includes bringing our full selves to the church, regardless of the stage of faith we are in (Simplicity, Complexity, Perplexity, or Harmony). I felt comfortable in the church when I was in Simplicity and Complexity because many of those around me were in those two stages also. I felt much less comfortable when I was in Perplexity, when I felt so much doubt, disillusionment, and suspicion.

Perplexity brought two feelings about church.

First, I felt that I did not belong. My stage of faith appeared—on the outside—so different from everyone else's, and what I needed to feel spiritually fed was different. I viewed myself as one of those optional organs—like an appendix or a gallbladder. Certainly I was part of the body, but the body would work fine if I wasn't there.

Second, when I was deep in Perplexity, I spent a lot of time at church internally criticizing what others were saying. I would hear echoes of a formulaic god or a simpler faith and wonder if the speaker had truly engaged with their faith. I worried that some of the things I heard would actually be harmful for many in the room if and when they reached Perplexity. I critiqued what I heard and often felt hurt because of it.

To reach a space where I felt like a necessary part of the church community—and where I viewed others in that community as necessary, also, despite their stage of faith—I adopted Elder Gerrit W. Gong's counsel to make church "a place of grace and space, where each can gather, with room for all."[3] And I followed Thomas Merton's guidance on communicating with others who are of different faiths: "Let not their Jesus be a barrier between us, or *they* will be a barrier between us and Jesus."[4] Everyone in the faith community was an important member *because of* their uniqueness, and that uniqueness strengthened the entire community, even if that uniqueness caused some bumps and bruises along the way.

"Imperfect people are all God has ever had to work with," Elder Jeffrey R. Holland directed. "That must be terribly frustrating to Him, but He deals with it."[5] I needed to learn to deal with it, too.

Dear people in my life modeled this graceful way of approaching church. After a session of general conference was over, I went on a walk with a dear friend who propped me up through this experience. She said that while she was listening to a talk, she felt some dissonance with what the speaker was saying and what she had experienced: the speaker had listed off promises and blessings for following a certain commandment, and she had not seen those blessings in her life despite following that same commandment. But she told me that she was able to hold space; in other words, she could allow the speaker to have his experience and beliefs, and at the same time, she could have her experiences, and she did not have to resolve the tension between the two. She could allow both of them to coexist beside each other without them being at war.

This friend modeled holding space: gently holding two things that appear to be contrary or opposite and not needing to resolve the tension between them.

Another time, when I thought I was making progress with giving grace and holding space, I sat in a Sunday School class when a classmate made a comment that I thought was completely contrary to everything that I was learning. I felt that this classmate's perception of the scriptures was overly narrow and therefore wrong. The next day, I talked with another dear friend who was in that class. I told her how that comment rubbed me the wrong way. And her response was that the comment was an answer to her prayer. What I find hard to hear might end up being an answer to someone else's prayer. It is quite possible for two people to hear the exact same comment and have one come away lifted and the other come away feeling dissatisfied.

President Henry B. Eyring counseled that differences in our church congregations "can be seen as an opportunity. God will help us see a difference in someone else not as a source of irritation but as a contribution. The Lord can help you see and value what another person brings which you lack."[6] Giving grace and holding space have allowed me to accept the diversity of faith stages at church. I can have my faith experiences without diminishing or exalting them, and those around me can have whatever experience they need to have. All of us are at different stages in our faith. My job is not to convince people to join me at the place where I am, but rather to support others wherever they may be.

My church community also taught me the meaning of the baptismal covenant to "mourn with those that mourn" and "comfort those that stand in need of comfort" (Mosiah 18:9). Never have those covenants meant more to me than during my quietness. And it was women in my Relief Society who blessed me by living their baptismal covenants.

I had been called as a teacher in Relief Society for a few months before the quietness started. I loved my calling. I loved teaching. I loved thinking about a gospel principle from a conference talk for several weeks before I taught. I loved thinking about what the women in my Relief Society needed.

I taught one lesson in January, when the quietness started, and then I did not teach for 10 months: a scheduling conflict prevented me from teaching in February, and in March, COVID-19 shut down church. My teaching responsibilities ceased while I walked through some of my darkest months.

In August, my Relief Society president asked if I could write a thought for the Relief Society newsletter that was based off of a recent conference talk. I knew I could not write about how wonderful COVID had been or how I had been reading the scriptures more because I had all this extra time or how I had felt God's peace in my life during that tumultuous time, because none of that was true for me. Instead, I pulled from Elder Neil L. Andersen's conference address where he talked about how our "spiritually defining memories from our book of life" can help "brighten the road ahead" when "personal difficulty, doubt, or discouragement darken our path."[7] I wrote that I had felt profound divine silence in response to earnest prayers, and that silence crumbled my faith. I wrote how I was hanging onto my spiritual memories as I was trying to rebuild my faith.

I sent a draft to my Relief Society president, letting her know that I could write something different if needed. She did not need something different. She sent out what I had written. I had several women reach out after they read it to give me encouragement and love. Two in particular changed my trajectory.

One invited me to go on a walk. For the first part of that walk, this friend listened as I unloaded my story. She wanted to hear it all. And for the second part, she told me how she had struggled with depression, and she wondered if depression had played a role in how I was feeling. She gently suggested that if I had any concerns, I might want to set an appointment with a therapist soon, because generally the wait list for a therapist was three months. That week, I made an appointment with a therapist, and—to be expected—the wait list was several months long. I continued walking with this friend, talking about mental health and the church and how to respond when we were disappointed by God.

Another friend reached out to me and said she had been experiencing similar quietness. We walked together as well, expressing our doubts, concerns, hopes, and confusion. We could say things out loud to each other that we did not feel comfortable saying in any other setting, because our space together was safe and born from shared pain. We would read books and listen to podcasts and then walk and talk about them. Sometimes we found satisfying answers to our questions. Many times we did not. Oftentimes we just supported each other through the quietness.

I walked with both of these women for miles talking about our confusion, why God's quietness was hurtful, what we wished we knew, and how we could stay with God despite our inclinations to walk away. I could say things in these conversations that I did not feel I could say elsewhere, because these women were experiencing what I was experiencing. They were safe. I was surprised that we could talk about our hard feelings and thoughts, and I still would come away from those conversations feeling lifted. And somehow, in the process of talking out loud about all my disappointment and hurt and surprise and resistance, those feelings lessened, and I could begin to heal.

These two women—and so many more who rallied around me and were willing to talk to me—helped me feel heard, seen, and loved. I could not feel God's love, but I could feel the love of those around me. And I wondered if God was showing his love to me by sending people into my life who could mourn with me.

Being willing to sit in uncomfortable places with those who are struggling—rather than finding the right answer for that struggling person—is the essence of living our baptismal covenants. At a BYU Women's Conference several years ago, Spencer Fluhman, the executive director of the Neal A. Maxwell Institute for Religious Scholarship, spoke about answering sincere gospel questions.[8] Often those who are answering questions are focused on their own insecurities and getting the answer right rather than on the person asking the question. He advocated for a more questioner-focused approach. By focusing on the questioner, the answerer can investigate whether the question is coming from a place of curiosity or pain, or a place of a new testimony or a dying one.

He also noted that those who have been baptized have made dual covenants to stand as a witness of God and to mourn with those that mourn. Although standing as a witness and bearing testimony is important, "using a testimony like Thor's hammer to smash a doubt or a skeptic is likely to end badly."[9]

Fluhman discussed an experience he had with a woman who had served a mission, loved God and the church, and was attracted to other women. Given the church's emphasis on families, the commandments, and her orientation, she asked him about what she was to do with the "suffocating loneliness" she felt. Fluhman stated that he felt the Spirit constrain him from giving an immediate answer to her question. Rather, after sitting in silence for a moment, he responded, "It seems to me that you are in mourning. You are mourning loss. And I am [bound by covenant] to mourn with you, so that is what I am going to do. I don't have an answer right now. I am just going to mourn with you, and then we will go from there."[10] He said that he and this woman are still talking about her questions, but they are doing so from a place of love and relationship.

THE BODY OF CHRIST

Connection and vulnerability are healing. When I was in a painful place of doubt and hurt—and when I got to a space where I was willing to share what I was feeling—by far the most helpful response was one of care and concern and mutual mourning. I did not need to hear testimonies at first. Many answers seemed too simple to fit what I had experienced. But I did need people to hear what I felt and acknowledge it. When that happened, I learned the power of the baptismal covenant to mourn with those who mourn more powerfully than I ever have in my life.

After I started the healing process, church became a place of much-needed pushing. I needed to learn to sit in church and hear everyone's experiences and hold space for their experiences and mine. I needed to hear things that helped me rethink some of my assumptions. I needed to learn to hear a comment—such as one that mentioned "doubters" in a derogatory way—and not take offense to it.

Starting to teach Relief Society again about eleven months after the quietness started helped with that push. I will forever be grateful to my Relief Society president who knew that I was struggling but still allowed me to teach. Teaching required me to dig back into conference talks and the scriptures and find themes that resonated with me that I could also teach to the women in my congregation. I wanted to teach from a place of genuineness, so I was determined to bring my full self to church, even the messy parts. That meant that I had to do the work to get myself in a space where I could teach appropriately and genuinely.

One of the first talks I was assigned to teach happened to be my least favorite talk from conference. It was centered on the scripture: "In the world ye shall have tribulation: but be of good cheer:

I have overcome the world" (John 16:33). I discussed the phrase "good cheer" with several people, wondering how I could genuinely teach about being of "good cheer" when I was still in the depths of a significant depression. Frankly, I wanted to punch anyone that told me to just be happy. Ultimately, I discovered in my concordance that the Greek word *tharseo* that is translated as "good cheer" in the King James Version of the Bible can also mean "to have courage."[11] In fact, other translations of the Bible translate that phrase: "But take courage."[12] I could talk about courage.

When the time came to teach, I told the women that I struggled with the phrase "good cheer" because I was struggling with depression. But the interpretation "have courage" resonated with me. I was having a hard time being happy, but I could have courage to move forward even in a dark place. We talked about scriptures where individuals moved forward with courage.

Those Relief Society lessons pushed me to challenge my assumptions and engage with talks or themes that I had avoided because they were uncomfortable. In fact, many of the ideas in this book sprang from preparing for a lesson. I am grateful for the loving push I felt in my calling.

In times of doubt and struggle, church can be a painful place. But it can also be a place where, as Elder Gerrit W. Gong puts it, we can "grow through our imperfect participation."[13] By participating in the body of Christ, I got to put into practice what I was learning: I had to learn to give grace, to hold space, to mourn with others (and to let others mourn with me), and to allow myself to be pushed. I strove to see those around me with Christlike love. Adam Miller defined this love beautifully: "In Christ, people and things can finally show up as being—perfectly—just whatever they are. No longer judging them in light of what I wanted them to be, I can actually see them. I can see their perfection. And, more, I can see what kind of care and healing they need. This is what life boils down to. This is what it means to love someone: *their obvious weakness cannot stop me from seeing their present perfection.*"[14]

This is the body that I want to be part of: A body whose members can truly see each other, who allow themselves to be truly seen, and still have great love for each other.

Foundation

The foundation of our spiritual life is oftentimes described as our testimony. I had often defined *testimony* narrowly: someone had a *testimony* if she received a spiritual manifestation that something was true, whether that be a feeling, a thought, a voice, peace, or something similar. I had seen the scriptures equate *testimony* with *knowledge*, and in my mind, *knowledge* required more than belief; it required a spiritual manifestation of truthfulness.

As you can imagine, that is a discouragingly high bar, especially for a person who is consumed in self-doubt about the inability to receive revelation. I wanted to believe, I desired to believe, I did believe, but I could not seem—for the vast majority of my "is this [fill in the blank] true" questions—to figure out a way to get a spiritual manifestation of truthfulness.

But my definition of *testimony* was not inclusive enough. In speaking about testimonies, Elder John K. Carmack offered a broader definition: "What does it mean to bear testimony? A testimony is an open declaration or confession of one's faith. To bear is to give or bring forward. So as I bear testimony, I am giving a declaration of my faith."[1]

A testimony is not just a statement of what I know, although that is what I often hear in church. Rather, a testimony can also be a statement of what I believe or even what I desire to believe. Testimony, simply defined, is an acknowledgment of our religious experience, whatever that experience has been. And it is important to remember, as Patrick Mason wrote, that in the bearing of testimonies "the commitment to live a religious life with integrity is related but not reducible to the act of having discernable 'spiritual experiences.'"[2] Thus, it is possible to think of a testimony as a "highly personalized reflection of a singular relationship between a unique eternal intelligence and God."[3] And that highly personalized reflection can include knowledge-type testimonies that come from strong spiritual experiences or believing-type testimonies that come from intent and desire.

About fourteen or fifteen months after my quietness started, I walked into sacrament meeting with my family on fast Sunday just as it was beginning. As it so happened, the closest available seat that I saw was on the front row. I sat down on the front bench, with the stairs leading up to the podium right in front of me. As I sat down, I had a feeling that I needed to bear my testimony. I had just written the paragraphs above and realized that it was possible that I did have a testimony despite it not being a knowledge-type testimony. But I was terrified at the thought of bearing my testimony. My faith felt fragile, and, quite frankly, I was a bit fragile too. Yet I felt the classic signs of the Spirit that I had longed for during the months prior, and I believed that if I wanted to show God that I was really interested in moving forward with him, I needed to get up and say whatever I could say.

So I got up and said that I had not received an answer I could recognize to many of the questions I had asked about the direction of my life or the truthfulness of many gospel principles. But I said that I had learned that a testimony did not have to be a knowledge one; it could come from belief or at least from desire. I said that I had desire, and I had hope. I sat down, exhausted.

Adam Miller defined a testimony as "a promise to stay."[4] He viewed a testimony as something that "gives form to your great faith" and also "gives direction to your great doubt" and "publicly commits you to the great effort of trying to live what God gives."[5] My testimony that day was a promise to stay. It gave words to what I was struggling with, and it gave power to my desire to continue to move forward. And by saying that publicly, I felt a combination of relief (that I was no longer hiding what I was feeling) and a deeper commitment to continue the wrestle. There is something about a public commitment that holds you tighter than a private commitment. Perhaps that is one reason why we have a testimony meeting once each month: it allows us to publicly express our faith, hopes, desires, and struggles, and in so doing, find deeper pools of strength and determination.

Several months after that testimony meeting, President Russell M. Nelson spoke in general conference about strengthening our faith. Strengthening faith has been a common theme for President Nelson. But this conference talk was different. Rather than giving a list of suggestions, he encouraged us to do whatever was necessary to build our faith. He prefaced this invitation, though, with a discussion about the extensive renovations to the foundation of the Salt Lake Temple. He drew an analogy between the strengthening happening at the Salt Lake Temple and the strengthening that he invited us to do on our own spiritual foundations.[6]

Interestingly enough, the renovations to the Salt Lake Temple's foundation are not simply patching up some loose mortar or fixing minor cracks. Rather, strengthening the temple against earthquakes and other weather events requires completely new elements that bring flexibility and strength to the temple.

The Salt Lake Temple was built between 1853 and 1893.[7] For the first two years, workers laid nearly 7,500 tons of roughly hewn stones to create the footings—part of the foundation—of the temple.[8] In 2015—122 years after the temple's completion—the Presiding Bishopric reviewed the temple and reported that although the temple was built using the best materials and engineering methods at the time, had been well maintained, and had strong floor joists and support beams, the temple's foundation could use a seismic upgrade.[9]

That upgrade began in 2020. After all the soil was removed to expose the foundation, the foundation was examined closely. In discussing that examination, President Nelson reported, "We can see the effects of erosion, gaps in the original stonework, and varying stages of stability in the masonry."[10] Although the foundation had been built with the best materials and methods available in the 1800s, time had weakened the foundation. And those weaknesses could only be fully assessed when the foundation was completely exposed.

The lengthy process to renovate the temple began with strengthening the existing foundation. Because the stones in the foundation were different sizes and in differing conditions, workers first drilled holes—anywhere from eight to thirty-five feet—horizontally through the foundation and pumped high-strength grout into those holes. Pumping that grout into the holes pushed the grout "into the voids and joints of the existing foundation stones, binding them together into a more cohesive structure."[11] Then the workers drilled new holes horizontally in the foundation and ran metal rods through those holes, giving the foundation even more strength.[12]

To strengthen the temple's towers and walls, workers drilled holes vertically through them, ran cables through those holes, and attached the cables to the foundation.[13]

Then began the process of installing a base isolation system, which will make the Salt Lake Temple earthquake resistant. When it was built, the temple's foundation was placed directly onto the ground, which meant that the foundation would move in whatever direction the ground moved; the temple was at the mercy of whatever forces came from the ground. However, a base isolation system detaches the building from the ground by placing base isolators between the building and the ground.

Base isolators look like enormous hockey pucks, and they work like shock absorbers.[14] These isolators do not touch each other; rather, they are placed at intervals underneath the foundation, and they allow the building to move in a slower and controlled manner.[15] For example, the Utah State Capitol's foundation was fitted with a base isolation system, and because of that system, the capitol can move two feet in any direction.[16]

The church's director for special projects, Brent Roberts, described the impact of the base isolation system on the temple's foundation and security: "We're decoupling the footings and foundation from the raw ground. . . . So it is the footings, foundation, base isolators and the ground. When an earthquake comes, depending upon the magnitude and depending upon the shaking, it follows that shaking in a very slowed-down manner. So the earth moves underneath, the base isolator stays still and they will gradually move at a certain parallel with the waves."[17]

Notably, the base isolation does not prevent the temple from moving; rather, the system acts as a buffer, allowing the temple to move in a slower and more controlled way. And with the additional strength that was given to the original foundation, towers, and walls, the entire temple can sway back and forth as a cohesive structure rather than snapping in half. The upgrade of the temple foundation has increased its strength (by pushing grout into the original foundation, adding metal rods to the original foundation, and connecting the walls and towers with cables) and added flexibility (by installing the base isolation system). Both strength and flexibility are necessary for the temple to withstand an earthquake.

In many ways, I have felt that the restructuring of my faith over the last several years has looked a lot like the renovation of the Salt Lake Temple's foundation. When I built my faith in my early life, I did the best I could with what I knew at the time. Although some of those ideas are no longer helpful to me, I can respect them for the faith they helped develop when I was younger.

As I have aged, my foundation was not as strong as I thought it was. My trust in God had eroded. I had avoided parts of the scriptures that I found distasteful or hard.

I thought rigidly about how God was supposed to show up in my life. My rigid faith did not have the strength to withstand the strong shaking that came from unmet expectations and divine quietness. It broke.

In the process of breaking and rebuilding, I had to excavate the thinking that had formed the foundation of my faith by asking a series of "why" questions. Once I fully saw those thoughts, I found many of those thoughts unhelpful. I had to let those go. I needed to replace my old, overly rigid foundation with things that were strong and flexible—my own base isolators. My base isolators needed to have gaps so that things could move—I could continue to rethink and grow—without the entire building collapsing. More and more, I have come to realize that my base isolators are Jesus. I needed to focus my faith and my spiritual strength on Jesus and on my conviction that Jesus is *good*. And then everything I built on top of my foundation needed to be connected back to Jesus, just as the towers in the Salt Lake Temple are connected by cables to the foundation.

Divine quietness has taught me that Jesus must be my focus. The core of my religious experience must be reserved for Jesus.

As I have been trying to focus more on Jesus, one of my favorite titles of his is Redeemer. While discussing this title, Wendy Ulrich noted that "God's greatest genius is His ability to turn the very worst things into the very best things."[18] That doesn't mean that God takes away pain, sickness, or evil. Rather, it means "He can teach us through the hardest things we experience some of life's most important lessons. . . . *It does mean He can redeem anything He allows to happen and turn it to some good. Sometimes great good.*"[19]

For me, that "some good" includes more humility, compassion, and nonjudgment. I am a different person today than I was before the quietness started. And that is a good thing.

Recently I compared letters I wrote to my children when they were seven years old. When my children are that age, I start studying the scriptures with them. To prepare for that studying, I create a scripture journal for them, and that journal begins with letters from my husband and me. Several years before the quietness began, I had written a letter to my son for his scripture journal, which contains a lot of "I know that . . ." and commendation about his good qualities. When it was time to create my daughter's journal nearly four years later, I was one year into my quiet period. The letter to my daughter was different. Rather than writing a lot of "I knows," I wrote a lot of "I hopes." Rather than talking about how her good qualities were a blessing, I mentioned that she had so many good qualities and that by coming to God, those good things would grow.

When I compare those letters, I see a person who has gone from ardent knowing to hoping and seeking for real internal change. I see a little more humility. And I see someone who realizes that too often we congratulate ourselves for our spiritual heights rather than focusing on God.

I do not feel that I have fully resolved the issues that instigated my crumbling faith. I have no additional clarity on how to receive divine answers to direct questions. Perhaps that piece of a spiritual life is off the table for me, or perhaps it is something that I will grow into. Despite that, I am learning to ask questions again. Along these lines, Susan H. Porter spoke about a dear family member who left the church because of unanswered questions. Decades later, after he spoke with close friends about his questions, he had the feeling "that God honored his questions and that not having clear answers should not stop him from moving forward."[20] I could move forward with God *even with* unanswered questions, as long as I had the conviction that God was good.

I am also seeing in the scriptures that God has a lot of questions for me. Jesus asks poignant questions throughout the Gospels: "What seek ye?" (John 1:38). "Believe ye that I am able to do this?" (Matthew 9:28). "Will ye also go away?" (John 6:67). "Whom say ye that I am?" (Matthew 16:15). "Wilt thou be made whole?" (John 5:6). In writing about these questions, S. Michael Wilcox reasoned, "Perhaps the critical point is that *God* has questions for *us* and we must wrestle—not to receive answers *from* Him, but to give them *to* Him. How we answer those questions tells our Father in Heaven much about us, and helps reveal ourselves to ourselves."[21] Perhaps part of Jesus's redemption of this experience has been allowing me to begin to see myself, truly.

I also see Jesus's redemption in the gift of being willing to wrestle. Lauren Winner recounted a comment a father made to his daughter when she expressed doubts about whether she should be confirmed into her church—confirmation being a mature, public affirmation of her faith. Her father told her, "What you promise when you are confirmed . . . is not that you will believe this forever. What you promise when you are confirmed is that *that* is the story you will wrestle with forever."[22]

Wrestling is in our faith lineage. As members of the church, we are part of the house of Israel. God changed Jacob's name to Israel after the two wrestled.

As told in the book of Genesis, Jacob was returning to his homeland to see his brother, Esau, after being away for many years. Given his history with Esau, Jacob was terrified that Esau would kill him and his family (see Genesis 32:7). The evening before he was to see Esau, Jacob isolated himself from his family and "there wrestled a man with him until the breaking of the day" (Genesis 32:24). That wrestle lasted all night long. Jacob clung to God, and God allowed Jacob to cling to him. Presumably God could have overpowered Jacob, but God chose to engage in the wrestle with Jacob.

At dawn, God gave Jacob a new name: Israel (see Genesis 32:28). As President Russell M. Nelson has pointed out, *Israel* means "let God prevail."[23] As we wrestle with God—as we engage with him as he engages with us—we can let God prevail in our lives. We can truly become Israel.

Although I felt for several months that God had left me entirely, in hindsight I see glimpses of God's hand during that dark period. I wonder if the thought to be a little vulnerable and share what I was feeling with a few people came from God. I wonder if those who listened to me without judgment and with compassion were God personified. I wonder if I was led to certain books that validated what I was feeling but also challenged my thinking and expanded my view.

I do feel that the thought to start writing was a prompt from God that came through my mother. And throughout this writing process, I have healed. I have seen God's hand more, clarified my thinking, and written down my most caustic thoughts, questioned them, and allowed them to leave.

I hope that I can continue to grow. I hope that I can feel compassion for the entire body of Christ: Those who are stalwart, those who are struggling, those who doubt. I hope to hold an intention to be open and to have a soft heart. I hope to catch myself if my heart begins to go cold. I hope to be less judgmental and more kind. I hope to focus more on Jesus. And I hope that as I turn my heart to Jesus, I can see him redeeming me.

Acknowledgments

I am grateful to be surrounded by supportive, wonderful people: my family, friends, work colleagues, neighborhood, and church community. Their kindness created space for me to write this book.

Celia Barnes and her team at Deseret Book gave this book life and expertly guided me through the submission and editing process.

My first readers gave invaluable feedback that improved the drafts and encouraged me to continue on: Becky Wright, Chance Thomas, Pamela Thomas, James McConkie, Judi McConkie, Sahra Affleck, Tiffany Orgill, Nancy Barrick, Kathleen Newman, Meggan Gonzalez, Alexandria Sandburg, Kristy Maxwell, Sally Holzer, and Ronda Goodell.

I sincerely appreciate the support of my family; they reviewed drafts and strengthened me: Doug and Cristy Robison, Roger and Patricia Adams, Dean and Kathleen Collinwood, Christopher and Marci Robison, Scott and Rachel Robison, Mary Robison, Jodi Riedthaler, Melanie Cook, Amanda Campos, and Michele Turner.

My children—Eli, Lizzy, and Maddy—gift me new perspectives and a zest for life. My life is richer because they are in it.

ACKNOWLEDGMENTS

My husband, Lucas, is my favorite human and biggest supporter. I am grateful for his incredible support and love.

And finally, I am grateful to God for giving me this experience and the strength to work through it.

Notes

Quietness

1. See, for example, Russell M. Nelson, "Revelation for the Church, Revelation for Our Lives," *Ensign*, May 2018; Russell M. Nelson, "Pure Truth, Pure Doctrine, and Pure Revelation," *Liahona*, November 2021.

Doubt

1. Citations to the Bible are to the King James Version. Some New Testament citations are from Thomas A. Wayment's translation, *The New Testament: A Translation for Latter-day Saints* (Salt Lake City and Provo, UT: Deseret Book and Religious Studies Center, 2018), and are identified by Wayment's name at the beginning of the parenthetical citation.
2. Jeffrey R. Holland, "Lord, I Believe," *Ensign*, May 2013, 94.
3. Dale G. Renlund, quoting John A. Widtsoe, in "Doubt Not, but Be Believing."
4. Dale G. Renlund, "Doubt Not, but Be Believing."
5. Brian D. McLaren, *Faith after Doubt*, xvi.
6. McLaren, *Faith after Doubt*, 45.
7. McLaren, *Faith after Doubt*, 95.
8. See McLaren, *Faith after Doubt*, 45–46.
9. McLaren, *Faith after Doubt*, 48.
10. See McLaren, *Faith after Doubt*, 48–49.
11. McLaren, *Faith after Doubt*, 61.
12. McLaren, *Faith after Doubt*, 67.

NOTES

13. See McLaren, *Faith after Doubt*, 66.
14. McLaren, *Faith after Doubt*, 69.
15. See McLaren, *Faith after Doubt*, 96.
16. McLaren, *Faith after Doubt*, 94.
17. McLaren, *Faith after Doubt*, 91.
18. See McLaren, *Faith after Doubt*, 124. McLaren built off the work of several others who studied developmental theory, including James W. Fowler. In 1981, Fowler published his seminal work, *Stages of Faith: The Psychology of Human Development and the Quest for Meaning*. He set out six stages of faith. Starting in stage three, faith progresses from seeing authority outside of self and being interested in conformity, questioning faith and authority structures, being comfortable that all questions cannot be easily found and recognizing the importance of a faith community, and reaching universalizing faith that allows the person to relate to those at any stage of faith.
19. McLaren, *Faith after Doubt*, 92.
20. See Thomas McConkie, *Navigating Mormon Faith Crisis*, 17.
21. McConkie, *Navigating Mormon Faith Crisis*, 18.
22. McConkie, *Navigating Mormon Faith Crisis*, 18.
23. McConkie, *Navigating Mormon Faith Crisis*, 18.
24. Dieter F. Uchtdorf, "Come, Join with Us," *Ensign*, November 2013, 23.
25. Adam S. Miller, *Letters to a Young Mormon*, 24.
26. Patrick O. Mason, *Planted*, 32.
27. Mason, *Planted*, 43.
28. Mason, quoting Romans 8:28, in *Planted*, 32.
29. McConkie, *Navigating Mormon Faith Crisis*, 83.

Rethinking

1. Russell M. Nelson, "We Can Do Better and Be Better," *Ensign*, May 2019, 67.
2. Adam Grant, *Think Again*, 4.
3. Grant, *Think Again*, 4.
4. Grant, *Think Again*, 60.
5. Grant, *Think Again*, 59.
6. Neil deGrasse Tyson, "The Scientific Method."
7. Tyson, "The Scientific Method."

NOTES

8. Thomas McConkie, *Navigating Mormon Faith Crisis*, 19.
9. C. S. Lewis, *A Grief Observed*, 66.
10. Jeffrey L. Thayne and Edwin E. Gantt, *Who Is Truth?* 67.
11. See James W. McConkie and Judith E. McConkie, *Whom Say Ye That I Am?* 76.

QUIETNESS, RETHOUGHT

1. Richard G. Scott, "Learning to Recognize Answers to Prayer," *Ensign*, November 1989, 31.
2. Terryl Givens and Fiona Givens, *Crucible of Doubt*, 117.
3. Givens and Givens, *Crucible of Doubt*, 33.
4. Dallin H. Oaks, "In His Own Time, In His Own Way," *Ensign*, August 2013, 22.
5. Dallin H. Oaks, "In His Own Time, In His Own Way," 22.
6. Lauren F. Winner, *Still*, 102, quoting Michael Rea, "Divine Hiddenness, Divine Silence."
7. Patrick O. Mason, *Planted*, 35.
8. Richard Rohr, *Falling Upward*, 144.
9. Adam S. Miller, *Letters to a Young Mormon*, 36.
10. Givens and Givens, *Crucible of Doubt*, 127.
11. Mother Teresa, *Come Be My Light*, 187.
12. Mother Teresa, *Come Be My Light*, 214.
13. Brian Kolodiejchuk, in *Come Be My Light*, 22.
14. Brian Kolodiejchuk, in *Come Be My Light*, 23.
15. Thomas Merton, *New Seeds of Contemplation*, 258.
16. Merton, *New Seeds of Contemplation*, 212.
17. Merton, *New Seeds of Contemplation*, 212.
18. Barbara Brown Taylor, *Learning to Walk in the Dark*, 145.
19. Taylor, *Learning to Walk in the Dark*, 145.
20. Peter Enns, *Sin of Certainty*, 167.
21. See Wendy Ulrich, *Let God Love You*, 24.
22. See Ulrich, *Let God Love You*, 26–34.
23. See Ulrich, *Let God Love You*, 35–36.
24. See Ulrich, *Let God Love You*, 36–38.
25. See Ulrich, *Let God Love You*, 38.
26. Ulrich, *Let God Love You*, 29.

NOTES

27. Ulrich, *Let God Love You*, 39.
28. Ulrich, *Let God Love You*, 40–41.
29. Ulrich, *Let God Love You*, 41.
30. Ulrich, *Let God Love You*, 42.
31. See Ulrich, *Let God Love You*, 31–33.
32. Ulrich, *Let God Love You*, 43.
33. Ulrich, *Let God Love You*, 44.

God's Will

1. Thomas Merton, *New Seeds of Contemplation*, 129.
2. Merton, *New Seeds of Contemplation*, 129.
3. Tom Christofferson, *A Better Heart*, 61.
4. D. Todd Christofferson, "Our Relationship with God," 78.
5. D. Todd Christofferson, "Our Relationship with God," 78.
6. Sheri Dew, "Sweet Above All That Is Sweet"; emphasis omitted.
7. Emily Belle Freeman, *Grace Where You Are*, 46.
8. Dew, "Sweet Above All That Is Sweet."
9. Adam S. Miller, *Future Mormon*, 2.
10. Miller, *Future Mormon*, 5.
11. Michael Austin, *Re-reading Job*, 90.
12. Amy A. Wright, "Christ Heals That Which Is Broken," *Liahona*, May 2022, 84.
13. Miller, *Future Mormon*, 24.
14. Terryl Givens and Fiona Givens, *Crucible of Doubt*, 78.
15. James E. Faulconer, *Thinking Otherwise*, 42–43.
16. Jeffrey R. Holland, "Waiting on the Lord," *Liahona*, November 2020, 116.
17. Jeffrey R. Holland, "Waiting on the Lord," 116.
18. Dieter F. Uchtdorf, "Fourth Floor, Last Door," *Ensign*, November 2016, 17.

Faith, Rethought

1. Dieter F. Uchtdorf, "He Will Place You on His Shoulders and Carry You Home," *Ensign*, May 2016, 103.
2. Russell M. Nelson, "Christ Is Risen; Faith in Him Will Move Mountains," *Liahona*, May 2021, 102; paragraphing altered.

NOTES

3. Dallin H. Oaks, "Desire," *Ensign*, May 2011, 42.
4. Neal A. Maxwell, "According to the Desire of [Our] Hearts," *Ensign*, November 1996.
5. Father Joseph Neuner, S.J., quoted in Mother Teresa, *Come Be My Light*, 216.
6. Jeffrey R. Holland, "Lord, I Believe," *Ensign*, May 2013, 94.
7. Brian D. McLaren, quoting Alan Watts, in *Faith after Doubt*, 117.
8. McLaren, *Faith after Doubt*, 117–18.
9. Lauren F. Winner, quoting Christopher Grasso, in *Still*, 169.
10. See Anthony Sweat, *Seekers Wanted*, 106.
11. Sweat, *Seekers Wanted*, 74.
12. Sweat, *Seekers Wanted*, 74.
13. Sweat, *Seekers Wanted*, 74.
14. Sweat, *Seekers Wanted*, 74.
15. Wendy Ulrich, *Let God Love You*, 18.
16. Ulrich, *Let God Love You*, 18.
17. Ulrich, *Let God Love You*, 19.
18. Jeffrey L. Thayne and Edwin E. Gantt, *Who Is Truth?* 64.

SPIRITUAL NOURISHMENT

1. Terryl Givens and Fiona Givens, *Crucible of Doubt*, 98.
2. Sheri Dew, *Worth the Wrestle*, 20; emphasis omitted.
3. Lynn G. Robbins, "Be 100 Percent Responsible," 1.
4. Peter Enns, *Sin of Certainty*, 58.
5. Enns, *Sin of Certainty*, 60.
6. Enns, *Sin of Certainty*, 60.
7. Rachel Held Evans, *Inspired*, 103.
8. Evans, *Inspired*, 104.
9. Anthony Sweat, *Seekers Wanted*, 56, quoting Steven C. Harper, "'That They Might Come to Understanding.'"
10. Sweat, *Seekers Wanted*, 59.
11. See Sweat, *Seekers Wanted*, 57.
12. Sweat, *Seekers Wanted*, 70.
13. Dallin H. Oaks, "Scripture Reading and Revelation," *Ensign*, January 1995.
14. Fiona Givens and Terryl Givens, *All Things New*, 66.

NOTES

15. Givens and Givens, *All Things New*, 67.
16. Russell M. Nelson, "Revelation for the Church, Revelation for Our Lives," *Liahona*, May 2018.
17. Dale G. Renlund, "Doubt Not, but Be Believing."
18. Lauren F. Winner, *Wearing God*, 17–18.
19. Winner, *Wearing God*, 247–48.
20. Wendy Ulrich, *Let God Love You*, x.
21. Thomas Merton, *New Seeds of Contemplation*, 224.
22. Merton, *New Seeds of Contemplation*, 224.
23. Jacob Z. Hess, Carrie Skarda, Kyle Anderson, and Ty Mansfield, *The Power of Stillness*, 55.
24. Hess et al., *Power of Stillness*, 53, quoting Thomas Keating, *Intimacy with God*, 17, 19, 43.
25. Hess et al., *Power of Stillness*, 18.
26. Ulrich, *Let God Love You*, 151.
27. Ulrich, *Let God Love You*, 152.
28. Ulrich, *Let God Love You*, 152.
29. Ulrich, *Let God Love You*, 153.
30. Ulrich, *Let God Love You*, 153.
31. Ulrich, *Let God Love You*, 15.
32. Winner, *Wearing God*, 57–58.
33. See *Saints, Volume 1: The Standard of Truth*, 89–99.
34. Dew, *Worth the Wrestle*, 12.
35. Rachel Held Evans, quoted in Brian D. McLaren, *Faith after Doubt*, 211.

THE BODY OF CHRIST

1. D. Todd Christofferson, "That They May Be One in Us," *Ensign*, November 2002, 73.
2. Anthony Sweat, *Seekers Wanted*, 123.
3. Gerrit W. Gong, "Room in the Inn," *Liahona*, May 2021, 25.
4. Thomas Merton, *New Seeds of Contemplation*, 107.
5. Jeffrey R. Holland, "Lord, I Believe," *Ensign*, May 2013, 94.
6. Henry B. Eyring, "Our Hearts Knit as One," *Ensign*, November 2008, 70–71.
7. Neil L. Andersen, "Spiritually Defining Memories," *Liahona*, May 2020, 21.

NOTES

8. See BYU Maxwell Institute, "Answering Sincere Gospel Questions with Spencer Fluhman."
9. BYU Maxwell Institute, "Answering Sincere Gospel Questions with Spencer Fluhman."
10. BYU Maxwell Institute, "Answering Sincere Gospel Questions with Spencer Fluhman."
11. James Strong, *New Strong's Expanded Exhaustive Concordance*, s.v. *"tharseo"* (Greek), word no. 2293.
12. The New Revised Standard Version translates this as: "In the world you face persecution. But take courage; I have conquered the world!" And the Berean Study Bible has it as: "In the world you will have tribulation. But take courage; I have overcome the world!"
13. Gerrit W. Gong, "Always Remember Him," *Ensign*, May 2016, 110.
14. Adam S. Miller, *An Early Resurrection*, 120–21; paragraphing altered.

FOUNDATION

1. John K. Carmack, "The Soil and Roots of Testimony," *Ensign*, November 1988, 25.
2. Patrick O. Mason, *Planted*, 27.
3. Mason, *Planted*, 27.
4. Adam S. Miller, *Letters to a Young Mormon*, 24.
5. Miller, *Letters to a Young Mormon*, 24.
6. See Russell M. Nelson, "The Temple and Your Spiritual Foundation," *Liahona*, November 2021, 93–96.
7. See Aubrey Eyre, "Lesser-Known Facts about Salt Lake Temple's Construction Illustrate Pioneers' Commitment, Sacrifice."
8. Paul C. Richards, "The Salt Lake Temple Infrastructure," 207.
9. See Gary E. Stevenson, "A Good Foundation against the Time to Come," *Liahona*, May 2020, 49.
10. Russell M. Nelson, "The Temple and Your Spiritual Foundation," *Liahona*, November 2021, 93.
11. "A Window Into Past, Present and Self."
12. "A Window Into Past, Present and Self."
13. See Tad Walch, "Updates announced for Salt Lake Temple renovation project."

NOTES

14. See Tad Walch, "Here's how the Salt Lake Temple's base isolation system will protect it from earthquakes."
15. Vasant A. Matsagar and R. S. Jangid, "Base Isolation for Seismic Retrofitting of Structures."
16. Walch, "Here's how the Salt Lake Temple's base isolation system will protect it from earthquakes."
17. Walch, "Here's how the Salt Lake Temple's base isolation system will protect it from earthquakes."
18. Wendy Ulrich, *Let God Love You*, 133.
19. Ulrich, *Let God Love You*, 133; emphasis added.
20. Susan H. Porter, "God's Love: The Most Joyous to the Soul," *Liahona*, November 2021, 34.
21. S. Michael Wilcox, *What Seek Ye?* 3.
22. Lauren F. Winner, *Still*, 172; emphasis added.
23. Russell M. Nelson, "Let God Prevail," *Liahona*, November 2020, 92.

Works Cited

Andersen, Neil L. "Spiritually Defining Memories." *Liahona*, May 2020.

Austin, Michael. *Re-reading Job: Understanding the Ancient World's Greatest Poem*. Sandy, UT: Greg Kofford Books, 2016.

BYU Maxwell Institute. *Answering Sincere Gospel Questions with Spencer Fluhman* (podcast). Available at https://mi.byu.edu/mip-fluhman/.

Carmack, John K. "The Soil and Roots of Testimony." *Ensign*, November 1988.

Christofferson, D. Todd. "Our Relationship with God." Available at https://www.churchofjesuschrist.org/study/general-conference/2022/04/41christofferson?lang=eng.

———. "That They May Be One in Us." *Ensign*, November 2002.

Christofferson, Tom. *A Better Heart: The Impact of Christ's Pure Love*. Salt Lake City: Deseret Book, 2020.

Dew, Sheri. "Sweet Above All That Is Sweet." *Y Magazine*. Available at https://magazine.byu.edu/article/sheri-dew-sweet-above-all-that-is-sweet/.

———. *Worth the Wrestle*. Salt Lake City: Deseret Book, 2017.

Enns, Peter. *The Sin of Certainty: Why God Desires Our Trust More Than Our "Correct" Beliefs*. New York: HarperOne, 2016.

Esplin, Scott C., Richard O. Cowan, and Rachel Cope, eds. *You Shall Have My Word: Exploring the Text of the Doctrine and Covenants*. Provo, UT, and Salt Lake City: Religious Studies Center and Deseret Book, 2012.

Evans, Rachel Held. *Inspired: Slaying Giants, Walking on Water, and Loving the Bible Again*. Nashville, TN: Thomas Nelson, 2018.

WORKS CITED

Eyre, Aubrey. "Lesser-Known Facts about Salt Lake Temple's Construction Illustrate Pioneers' Commitment, Sacrifice," 17 May 2019. Available at https://www.churchofjesuschrist.org/church/news/lesser-known-facts-about-salt-lake-temples-construction-illustrate-pioneers-commitment-sacrifice?lang=eng.

Eyring, Henry B. "Our Hearts Knit as One." *Ensign*, November 2008.

Faulconer, James E. *Thinking Otherwise: Theological Explorations of Joseph Smith's Revelations*. Provo, UT: BYU Maxwell Institute, 2020.

Fowler, James W. *Stages of Faith: The Psychology of Human Development and the Quest for Meaning*. New York: HarperOne, 1981.

Freeman, Emily Belle. *Grace Where You Are*. Salt Lake City: Deseret Book, 2020.

Givens, Fiona, and Terryl Givens. *All Things New: Rethinking Sin, Salvation, and Everything in Between*. Faith Matters, 2020.

Givens, Terryl, and Fiona Givens. *The Crucible of Doubt: Reflections on the Quest for Faith*. Salt Lake City: Deseret Book, 2014.

Gong, Gerrit W. "Always Remember Him." *Ensign*, May 2016.

———. "Room in the Inn." *Liahona*, May 2021.

Grant, Adam. *Think Again: The Power of Knowing What You Don't Know*. New York: Viking, 2021.

Harper, Steven C. "'That They Might Come to Understanding': Revelation as Process." In *You Shall Have My Word*, 19–33.

Hess, Jacob Z., Carrie Skarda, Kyle Anderson, and Ty Mansfield. *The Power of Stillness: Mindful Living for Latter-day Saints*. Salt Lake City: Deseret Book, 2019.

Holland, Jeffrey R. "Lord, I Believe." *Ensign*, May 2013.

———. "Waiting on the Lord." *Liahona*, November 2020.

Keating, Thomas. *Intimacy with God: An Introduction to Centering Prayer*. New York: Crossroad Publishing, 2009.

Lewis, C. S. *A Grief Observed*. New York: HarperCollins, 1996.

Mason, Patrick O. *Planted: Belief and Belonging in an Age of Doubt*. Salt Lake City: Deseret Book, 2015.

Matsagar, Vasant A., and R. S. Jangid. "Base Isolation for Seismic Retrofitting of Structures," *Practice Periodical on Structural Design and Construction* 175 (November 2008). Available at https://www.researchgate.net/profile/Vasant-Matsagar/publication/245492481_Base_Isolation_for_Seismic_Retrofitting_of_Structures/links/541890fb0cf2218008bf409b/Base-Isolation-for-Seismic-Retrofitting-of-Structures.pdf.

Maxwell, Neal A. "According to the Desire of [Our] Hearts." *Ensign*, November 1996.

McConkie, James W., and Judith E. McConkie. *Whom Say Ye That I Am? Lessons from the Jesus of Nazareth*. Sandy, UT: Greg Kofford Books, 2018.

McConkie, Thomas Wirthlin. *Navigating Mormon Faith Crisis: A Simple Developmental Map*, second edition. Salt Lake City: Mormon Stages, 2015.

McLaren, Brian D. *Faith after Doubt: Why Your Beliefs Stopped Working and What to Do about It*. New York: St. Martin's, 2021.

Merton, Thomas. *New Seeds of Contemplation*. New York: New Directions, 2007.

Miller, Adam S. *An Early Resurrection: Life in Christ before You Die*. Salt Lake City: Deseret Book, 2018.

———. *Future Mormon: Essays in Mormon Theology*. Sandy, UT: Greg Kofford Books, 2016.

———. *Letters to a Young Mormon*, second edition. Salt Lake City: Deseret Book, 2017.

Mother Teresa. *Come Be My Light: The Private Writings of the Saint of Calcutta*. Edited by Brian Kolodiejchuk. New York: Image, 2007.

Nelson, Russell M. "Christ Is Risen; Faith in Him Will Move Mountains." *Ensign*, May 2021.

———. "Let God Prevail." *Liahona*, November 2020.

———. "Revelation for the Church, Revelation for Our Lives." *Liahona*, May 2018.

———. "The Temple and Your Spiritual Foundation." *Liahona*, November 2021.

———. "We Can Do Better and Be Better." *Ensign*, May 2019.

Oaks, Dallin H. "Desire." *Ensign*, May 2011.

———. "In His Own Time, In His Own Way." *Ensign*, August 2013.

WORKS CITED

———. "Scripture Reading and Revelation." *Ensign*, January 1995.

Porter, Susan H. "God's Love: The Most Joyous to the Soul." *Liahona*, November 2021.

Rea, Michael, and Louis P. Pojman. "Divine Hiddenness, Divine Silence." In *Philosophy of Religion: An Anthology*. Belmont, CA: Wadsworth, 2011.

Renlund, Dale G. "Doubt Not, but Be Believing." Worldwide Devotional for Young Adults, 13 January 2019. Available at https://www.churchofjesuschrist.org/broadcasts/article/worldwide-devotionals/2019/01/11renlund?lang=eng.

Richards, Paul C. "The Salt Lake Temple Infrastructure: Studying It Out in Their Minds," *BYU Studies Quarterly*, vol. 36, no. 2 (1996). Available at https://scholarsarchive.byu.edu/byusq/vol36/iss2/12.

Robbins, Lynn G. "Be 100 Percent Responsible." Brigham Young University devotional, 22 August 2017. *Speeches.BYU.edu* (website). Available at https://speeches.byu.edu/talks/lynn-g-robbins/be-100-percent-responsible/.

Rohr, Richard. *Falling Upward: A Spirituality for the Two Halves of Life*. San Francisco: Jossey-Bass, 2011.

Saints: The Story of the Church of Jesus Christ in the Latter Days. Volume 1: The Standard of Truth, 1815–1846. Salt Lake City: The Church of Jesus Christ of Latter-day Saints, 2018.

Scott, Richard G. "Learning to Recognize Answers to Prayer." *Ensign*, November 1989.

Stevenson, Gary E. "A Good Foundation against the Time to Come." *Liahona*, May 2020.

Strong, James. *The New Strong's Expanded Exhaustive Concordance of the Bible: Red Letter Edition*. Nashville, TN: Thomas Nelson, 2001.

Sweat, Anthony. *Seekers Wanted*. Salt Lake City: Deseret Book, 2019.

Taylor, Barbara Brown. *Learning to Walk in the Dark*. New York: HarperOne, 2014.

Thayne, Jeffrey L., and Edwin E. Gantt. *Who Is Truth? Reframing Our Questions for a Richer Faith*. Verdand Press, 2019.

WORKS CITED

Tyson, Neil deGrasse. "Chapter 3: The Scientific Method," *Neil deGrasse Tyson Teaches Scientific Thinking and Communication*. Masterclass.com (website).

Uchtdorf, Dieter F. "Come, Join with Us." *Ensign*, November 2013.

———. "Fourth Floor, Last Door." *Ensign*, November 2016.

———. "He Will Place You on His Shoulders and Carry You Home." *Ensign*, May 2016.

Ulrich, Wendy. *Let God Love You: Why We Don't, How We Can*. Salt Lake City: Deseret Book, 2016.

Walch, Tad. "Here's how the Salt Lake Temple's base isolation system will protect it from earthquakes." *Deseret News*, 19 April 2019. Available at https://www.deseret.com/2019/4/19/20671272/here-s-how-the-salt-lake-temple-s-base-isolation-system-will-protect-it-from-earthquakes.

———. "Updates announced for Salt Lake Temple renovation project." *Deseret News*, 13 December 2021. Available at https://www.deseret.com/faith/2021/12/13/22832545/salt-lake-temple-renovation-now-expected-to-be-completed-in-2025-first-presidency-says.

Wayment, Thomas A. *The New Testament: A Translation for Latter-day Saints*. Salt Lake City and Provo, UT: Deseret Book and Religious Studies Center, 2018.

"A Window Into Past, Present and Self: Salt Lake Temple Renovation Enters the Foundation-Strengthening Phase: Sealing addition, north entrance, and underground facilities removed to make way for extensive excavation." *Church Newsroom*, 25 September 2020. Available at https://newsroom.churchofjesuschrist.org/article/salt-lake-temple-renovation-update-september-2020.

Winner, Lauren F. *Still: Notes on a Mid-Faith Crisis*. New York: HarperOne, 2012.

———. *Wearing God: Clothing, Laughter, Fire, and Other Overlooked Ways of Meeting God*. New York: HarperOne, 2015.

Wilcox, S. Michael. *What Seek Ye? How the Questions of Jesus Lead Us to Him*. Salt Lake City: Deseret Book, 2020.

Wright, Amy A. "Christ Heals That Which Is Broken." *Liahona*, May 2022.